# THE
# CANNABIS COMPANION

# THE
# CANNABIS COMPANION

## THE ULTIMATE GUIDE TO CONNOISSEURSHIP

*by Steven Wishnia*

RUNNING PRESS

Library of Congress  Control Number: 2004090701

ISBN 0-7624-2149-5

This book was created by
THE IVY PRESS LTD
The Old Candlemakers
West Street, Lewes
East Sussex BN7 2NZ

creative director  Peter Bridgewater
publisher  Sophie Collins
editorial director  Jason Hook
senior project editor  Caroline Earle
designer  Clare Barber
illustrations  Coral Mula
studio photography  Ian Parsons
picture research  Lynda Marshall

**Publisher's Note**
We take great care to ensure that the information included in this book is accurate and
presented in good faith, but no warranty is provided nor results guaranteed. This material is intended
for informational and entertainment purposes only. The publisher does not condone illegal activity of any kind.

This book may be ordered by mail from the publisher. Please include $2.50 for postage and handling.
But try your bookstore first!

Running Press Book Publishers
125 South Twenty-second Street
Philadelphia, Pennsylvania 19103-4399
Visit us on the web!
www.runningpress.com

# CONTENTS

# INTRODUCTION

Cannabis has been part of human culture for at least 10,000 years, since the fibers of the plant's stalk were first woven into hemp fabric. It's been used for cloth, paper, food, medicine, religious trances, and, most notoriously, to get high, stoned, baked, lifted, buzzed, or *ido* (gone).

Today it's grown all over the world, from the hydroponic gardens of the Netherlands to the mountains of British Columbia, from the redwood forests of California's Humboldt County to the Gulf Stream waters of Florida. It's smoked in Swaziland and Switzerland, New York and New Guinea. It's consumed by illiterates and intellectuals, Indian mystics and Afghani soldiers, Jamaican shantytown dwellers and Silicon Valley computer millionaires. It's called *dagga* in South Africa and *mota* in Mexico, *pakalolo* in Hawaii and *chocolat* in Spain, "herb" by reggae fans and "trees" by hip-hop heads.

Much writing, art, and music has been created by avid marijuana users, especially in the last 170 years. Just try to imagine 20th-century music without Louis Armstrong, the Beatles, and Bob Marley! Medical users swear it helps them cope with multiple sclerosis, AIDS, and chronic pain. Recent research has found a system of natural cannabinoids in the brain, and what these do is just being discovered.

Yet cannabis has been denounced for centuries as a cause of subversion and perversion, indolence and irrational violence. Despite official tolerance in a few countries, most prominently the Netherlands, there is nowhere in the world where it's completely legal, and at least three nations have the death penalty for pot dealers. As cannabis is certainly no more harmful than alcohol, finding a rational justification for prohibition is difficult. The true reason is probably cultural war. "Christianity and capitalism are probably right to detest a plant like cannabis," writes Michael Pollan in *The Botany of Desire*. By offering sensory pleasures and "something like fulfillment" in the present, he contends, it undermines the belief that fulfillment should come from either future salvation or buying things. Or as comedian Lenny Bruce gibed, it's because the only reason to smoke pot is "To Serve the Devil—Pleasure!" On the other hand, plenty of Christians get high, and cannabis is a lucrative leisure commodity that also stimulates the markets for CDs, movies, and pizza delivery.

The laws *are* enforced. In the five years from 1998 to 2003, about 3 million Americans were arrested simply for possessing cannabis. The drug laws have been a convenient way to jail racial minorities and social deviants.

Why shouldn't people be able to go to a store and choose between a sweet, uplifting sativa and a spicy, mellow indica, in the same way wine drinkers can pick a French Beaujolais or a California cabernet? Why can't people go out to a cannabis coffeeshop as legally as they go to a bar, as long as they're old enough and don't drive while wasted? The current U.S. rulers fight wars to protect rich Americans' privileges to drive pollution-spewing behemoths—and a "drug war" against an emaciated AIDS patient lighting up a skinny little pinner.

I had my first encounter with cannabis in 1969, when I copped a $5 bag of dubious quality on a Saturday-afternoon trip to New York's Greenwich Village. Since then, I've found it fun for some things, useful for others, and deleterious when used stupidly or excessively. I've enjoyed writing this exploration of the herb's history, science, and botany, and I hope you find it entertaining, exciting, and enlightening.

And I still get high, and I'm sick and tired of being treated like a criminal.     *Steven Wishnia, January 2004*

# CULTURAL HISTORY

*"Russell Dreck sat in his room in a hypnotic trance,
unaware that the cobwebs in the plant his mother
had given him for Easter had gotten out of hand.
He sat there dejected, listless, pepless,
and—the most tragic of all to a warped mind—potless."*

Lenny Bruce, Stamp Help Out, 1960

*"Persons using this narcotic, smoke the dried leaves of the
plant, which has the effect of driving them completely
insane.... Addicts to this drug, while under its
influence...become raving maniacs and are liable to
kill or indulge in any form of violence to other persons,
using the most savage methods of cruelty without
any sense of moral responsibility."*

Los Angeles Police Chief Charles A. Jones, in a letter to Canadian Judge Emily Murphy, 1922

*"Straight people don't know what you're about."*

Black Sabbath, "Sweet Leaf," 1971

# THE VENERABLE HERB
# CANNABIS IN ANTIQUITY

Cannabis first appears in history in Taiwan, around 8000 BCE, in shards of pots that had been decorated with twists of hemp fiber. The first written mention of it is from 2737 BCE in China, as a medicine, by Emperor Shen Nung.

🌿 *In the 5th century BCE, the Scythians burned buds like these inside tents and inhaled the smoke.*

A legendary figure, Emperor Shen Nung was also credited with the discovery of ginseng, ephedra, and caffeinated tea. His guide to herbs, passed down through the ages, recommended *ma* (cannabis) for constipation, rheumatism, menstrual cramps, and absentmindedness. A later edition said eating too many seeds could make you "see demons" or "communicate with the spirits." *Ma* was China's staple fiber crop, and was used for the first paper, around the 1st century BCE. In the 2nd century CE, surgeon Hua T'o used a hashish-wine concoction as an anesthetic.

In India, cannabis was used for medicine and religious intoxication. The *Atharva Veda*, a sacred text on the "science of charms" written between 2000 and 1400 BCE, praised it as one of the herbs that "release us from anxiety." Indians developed three main forms of cannabis—*bhang*, a drink made from the herb, milk, sugar, nuts, and spices; *ganja*, the buds and top leaves; and *charas*, the resin, hashish—which have remained in religious and social use to this day. Legend holds that the Hindu god Shiva, the "Lord of Bhang," discovered the cannabis plant and brought it down from the Himalayas.

🌿 *Fifteenth-century bronze sculpture depicting Shiva Nataraja, the Hindu god believed to have discovered cannabis, "the Poor Man's Heaven."*

By the millennium before the birth of Christ, cannabis had spread to central Asia and Europe. The Scythians, a nomadic, bloodthirsty (literally) warrior tribe that lived on the northern shores of the Black Sea, are the first recorded inhalers. After funerals, the Greek historian Herodotus wrote sometime around 440 BCE, they would build a small tent with a dish of red-hot stones inside. "They take some hemp seed, creep into the tent, and throw the seed onto the hot stones. At once it begins to smoke, giving off a vapor unsurpassed by any vapor-bath one could find in Greece. The Scythians enjoy it so much they howl with pleasure." This practice, along with the Scythians' grisly royal funeral rites, was confirmed in 1929 when a Soviet archeologist found charred seeds in a tomb. It's likely that the Scythians were burning buds, and the seeds are what remained. A nearby people, the Thracians, burned pot on campfires.

The Scythians also gave the world the word "cannabis." Some people have argued that the ancient Hebrew word "qeneh" or "kaneh bosm," translated in the Bible as "calamus" or "sweet cane," is really cannabis. However, Ernest L. Abel, in *Marihuana: The First 12,000 Years*, contends that *qeneh* is described as a sweet-tasting spice, so it's more likely sugar. In 1993, Israel was the site of the first archeological discovery of preserved hashish: traces were found in the tomb of a 14-year-old girl who died in childbirth around 390 CE.

Hashish spread through the Muslim world in the Middle Ages, probably brought from India. Unlike alcohol, it is not explicitly forbidden by the Koran. Haidar, founder of one sect of the Sufis, a mystical tradition within Islam, is credited with discovering it in 1155, by eating the leaves of a dancing plant. However, a doctor named Ibn Wahshiyah had warned of its dangers—grossly exaggerating them—more than a century before. In 13th-century Egypt, the Garden of Cafour in Cairo was a

*Eighteenth-century Indian miniature painting of fakirs preparing ganja and the cannabis drink bhang.*

favorite hashish-eaters' haunt. Three attempts were made to suppress the drug between 1253 and 1378, with sanctions such as executing growers and pulling the teeth of users. They failed.

The tales of the "hashishins," the deadly followers of 11th-century warlord Hasan-ibn-Sabah, are shrouded in legend. The usual version is that Hasan used *hashish*, scantily clad maidens, and talking-head actors buried up to their neck in bloody sand to create a vision of paradise and heroic duty for his minions. But the word "assassin" may actually come from the Arabic for "kill"—*hassas*. Hashish also figures in several stories in *1001 Nights*—"Art thou not ashamed, O Hashish-eater, to be sleeping stark naked with stiff-standing tool?"

Cannabis also arrived on the east coast of Africa in the Middle Ages, either brought

*A hookah, a traditional Turkish waterpipe. Hashish spread through the Muslim world in the Middle Ages.*

from India by Arab traders or carried back from Egypt. Used waterpipe bowls dating to about 1320 were found in Ethiopia in 1971. By the 17th century in southern Africa, the Hottentots, Bushmen, and Zulus all smoked *dagga*, sometimes in pipes dug out of mounds of earth. The Bashilange, a Congolese people, turned from warriors to pacifists after they began worshipping *riamba*, according to a 19th-century German explorer. Bashilange guilty of crimes had to smoke until they passed out.

In Europe, the Roman physician Galen recommended cannabis to kill pain and limit flatulence. The Romans, the Vikings, and the ancient French grew hemp for cloth and rope, and large-scale production of hemp began in Italy in the Middle Ages. However, there are relatively few references in European history to the use of cannabis for anything but hemp. Witches used it in rituals, and Pope Innocent VIII denounced it as satanic in 1484. Peasants in Poland and Russia used it to relieve the pain of toothaches and childbirth. In the 16th century, Garcia Da Orta, a closet-Jewish doctor who practiced in the Portuguese colony of Goa, described the effects of bhang and noted that the colonists were using it too. In 1680, English sea captain

*There is no known record of the Romans smoking cannabis, but they grew it for hemp and used it as medicine.*

Thomas Bowrey wrote of drinking bhang in India. One of his mates stuck his head in a jar for four hours, but several others were each "fancyinge himslefe noe less than an emperor."

Spain cultivated hemp in the New World almost immediately after the conquests of the 16th century. It was grown in Chile in 1545 to make rope and rigging for the Spanish army and navy there, and may have been brought to Mexico in 1530 by Pedro Cuadrado, one of Hernan Cortez's conquistadors. In 1550, according to Ernest Abel, Mexico's governor ordered Cuadrado and his partner to reduce production "because the natives were beginning to use the plants for something other than rope." Others speculate that pot-smoking came over with the Spanish, from the Moorish tradition of North African-style kif-toking.

There is some evidence that slaves imported from Angola brought it to Brazil. Others argue that it's more likely that the Portuguese brought it for hemp, and the African slaves smoked it. The city of Rio de Janeiro banned *maconha* in 1830, with three days in jail for any slaves caught puffing.

In the US, hemp was cultivated in Virginia in 1611, less than five years after the first permanent settlement at Jamestown. It required some arm-twisting from British authorities, as it was not as profitable a crop as tobacco. Most of

Virginia's hemp was sent to New England's "ropewalks" for use in ships. Thomas Jefferson advocated growing it, and George Washington's diary notations from 1765— "Sowed Hemp at Muddy hole by Swamp" and then the cryptic "began to separate the Male from the Female Hemp… rather too late"—are favorites of stoner lore: "George Washington was growing *sinsemilla*, man!" But that's unlikely, as there is almost no evidence that more than a few people in the Western world used pot to get high before 1800. That would change within a few decades.

🌿 *Hemp farmer George Washington. Washington's diary entry about separating the males from the females is followed by notations about retting the stalks in the river, indicating he was growing it for rope.*

# THE WEST GETS HIGH

Blame it on Napoleon. When he invaded Egypt in 1798, there was no alcohol available for his soldiers, so they turned to the local hashish. Napoleon tried to ban it in 1800, with about as much success as other attempts at pot prohibition. Three scientists attached to the French army brought some back for further experiments. By the 1830s, youths in the port of Marseilles were using Egyptian hashish "as a frolic."

In the 1840s, French psychologist Dr. Jacques-Joseph Moreau used hashish in research, attempting to cure depression and simulate psychosis. Dr. Moreau was also the source for the Club des Hashischins, a group of writers who met monthly in a decayed elegant hotel in Paris' Latin Quarter to eat a green hashish paste called dawamesk. Organized by Théophile Gautier, the group included Gerard de Nerval, Alexandre Dumas, Victor Hugo, Charles Baudelaire, and Honoré de Balzac, though Balzac usually preferred to observe. Later, poet Arthur Rimbaud would use hashish to seek visions from "the derangement of the senses."

❧ *Napoleon's soldiers introduced hashish to Europe after the 1798 invasion of Egypt.*

"The hashish spreads over all the world like a magic glaze," Baudelaire rhapsodized in *Artificial Paradise*. "Craggy countrysides, receding horizons, city vistas whitened by the ghastly lividity of a storm, or lit by the dense heat of setting suns." Still, he concluded, if paradise could be found in a single spoonful of green jelly, no one would work, and there would be "that terrible Morning After."

In Britain and the United States, cannabis preparations were used in both legitimate and patent medicines after the 1840s. Some of this was diverted. American writer Fitz Hugh Ludlow, author of *The Hasheesh Eater*, acquired his from a drugstore. Like Baudelaire, he experienced both rapture and nightmare. By 1880, there were "hashish parlors" in New York and other US cities, exotically decorated with violet cloth and beaded curtains.

Jamaica's ganja genesis came from Indian indentured workers imported after the end of slavery in 1838. In Mexico after

## Hashish Club of Paris

After eating a thumb-size piece of hashish paste, Théophile Gautier hallucinated "hodgepodges of spangles and rags of human and bestial figures," but "good humor alone uncovered their jagged fangs and sharp incisors....to mutter in my ear banter, none of which I now remember, but which, at the time, I found prodigiously witty."

the revolution of 1910, "La Cucaracha" was the anthem of Pancho Villa's peasant army. "La cucaracha, la cucaracha, ya no puede caminar, porque no tiene, porque le falta, marijuana que fumar." (The cockroach can't walk because it has no marijuana to smoke.) Pot's permanent entry to the US came around 1900, via Mexican immigrants in Texas and sailors who brought marijuana back from Mexico and Central America. Puerto Rican soldiers in Panama were recorded smoking it in 1916. Pot took root in the port of New Orleans, where black laborers and the musicians of the city's burgeoning jazz scene adopted it.

Like jazz, it came up the river in the 1920s. New York's Harlem neighborhood, the cultural capital of Black America, was

the epicenter of the jazz-and-jive scene of the 1930s, with scores of "tea pads," apartments with colored lights and record players catering to "vipers"—so named for the serpentine hiss of toking up.

White jazz fans were picking up on it, too. For a working-class Jewish youth making $8 a week during the Depression, recalled viper Bernie Brightman in Larry Sloman's book *Reefer Madness*, a marvelous Saturday night out was 10 cents for subway fare, 20 cents to get into the Savoy Ballroom in Harlem, and a quarter for three reefers. At dances in Brooklyn's Brighton Beach neighborhood, he said, "fifty guys would be passing joints... Can you imagine that kind of scene in 1939?"

*New York's Harlem neighborhood was the capital of the 1930s jazz scene, with parties where "everybody blew gage and juiced back and jumped."*

# THE DEMON WEED
## MARIJUANA PROHIBITION

"If the hideous monster Frankenstein came face to face with the monster marihuana, he would drop dead of fright," thundered Harry Anslinger, head of the Federal Bureau of Narcotics, in 1937. His scare propaganda looks ludicrous today, but fueled by racism and puritanism, it led to the prohibition of cannabis in the USA and ultimately the world.

🌿 Harry Anslinger, head of the Federal Bureau of Narcotics, declared marijuana to be more frightening than Frankenstein in his 1930s scare propaganda.

The first modern countries to ban cannabis both had white minorities ruling black majorities: South Africa in 1911 and Jamaica, then a British colony, in 1913. Britain added cannabis to its list of illegal narcotics in the 1920s, as did New Zealand.

In the United States, marijuana prohibition began in the South and Southwest, where blacks and Mexican immigrants were smoking it. The Texas border city of El Paso outlawed it in 1914, followed by California in 1915, Texas in 1919, and Louisiana in 1924. A 1931–32 study of US soldiers in Panama concluded that the majority of pot-smokers were "morons and psychopaths," but "No mental or physical deterioration effects of smoking mariajuana could be demonstrated."

The campaign against cannabis heated up in the 1930s. "I wish I could show you what a small marihuana cigaret can do to one of our degenerate Spanish-speaking residents," a Colorado newspaper editor wrote in 1936. "The fatal marihuana cigarette must be recognized as a DEADLY DRUG and American children must be PROTECTED AGAINST IT," the Hearst newspaper chain editorialized. In 1936, 18 states outlawed pot.

## Marijuana Movies

Several films exploited the scare, including *Marihuana: The Weed With Roots in Hell, Assassin of Youth*, and, most notoriously, *Reefer Madness*. In *Reefer Madness*, an absurdly wholesome ("gosh, swell, Mom") group of high-school students plummets into an abyss of sex, suicide, insanity, and murder after smoking reefers. One character looks as bug-eyedly demented as Victor Licata's mugshot. Yet in a plot string left untied, the stoned hit-run driver who kills an old man gets away unmolested.

🌿 *Misery and "weird orgies": Poster for the 1930s movie* Marihuana: Weed with Roots in Hell.

🌿 *Sensational newspaper horror stories paved the way for prohibition.*

Anslinger headed the charge. An ambitious racist (a 1934 memo described an informant as a "ginger-colored nigger") who had been a hardline Prohibition official in the 1920s, he railed against reefer in magazine articles like 1937's "Marihuana: Assassin of Youth." This featured gory stories like that of Victor Licata, a once "sane, rather quiet young man" from Tampa, Florida who had killed his family with an axe in 1933, after becoming "pitifully crazed" from smoking "muggles." (Actually, the Tampa police had tried to have Licata committed to a mental hospital before he started smoking pot.)

Anslinger's other theme was that white girls would be ruined once they'd experienced the lurid pleasures of having a black man's joint in their mouth. "Colored students at the Univ. of Minn. partying with female students (white) smoking and getting their sympathy with stories of racial persecution," he noted. "Result pregnancy."

His Canadian counterpart was Emily F. Murphy, a feminist but racist judge who wrote anti-Asian, anti-marijuana screeds under the pseudonym "Janey Canuck." Canada added cannabis to its narcotics-prohibition law in 1923, several years before there were any reports of people actually smoking it there.

In 1937, after a very cursory debate in Congress, the United States enacted the Marihuana Tax Act, levying a prohibitive

A MAJOR INFLUENCE IN FORMING THE ATTITUDES THAT LED TO THE PRESENT LEGAL SITUATION REGARDING MARIJUANA ... HILARIOUS WHEN VIEWED FROM THE OTHER SIDE OF THE GENERATION GAP, A GAP THIS FILM DID SO *!!?H TO CREATE

THE NATIONAL ORGANIZATION FOR THE REFORM OF MARIJUANA LAWS

*presents*

# MARIJUANA
## WEED FROM THE DEVIL'S GARDEN!

One MOMENT of BLISS — A LIFETIME of REGRET!

"*Reefer*" MADNESS

HUNTING A THRILL, THEY INHALED A DRAG OF CONCENTRATED SIN!

A NORML FILM

WAKE UP AMERICA! HERE'S A ROADSIDE WEED THAT'S FAST BECOMING A NATIONAL HIGH-WAY!

🌿 *Ad for* Reefer Madness, *the 1930s pot-scare film that became a camp favorite among stoners in the 1970s.*

$100-an-ounce tax on cannabis. The law didn't ban medical use, but cannabis was removed from the US pharmacopoeia in 1941.

Many people, most notably hemp activist Jack Herer, believe that marijuana prohibition was a Hearst–DuPont corporate conspiracy to eliminate hemp as competition for wood-pulp paper and synthetic fabrics. That is unlikely. Newspaper magnate William Randolph Hearst may have had substantial forest investments, but his papers never needed an excuse to trumpet fiendish menaces, from Spain in 1898 to communists in 1948. In his book *The*

*Emperor Wears No Clothes*, Herer argues that the DuPont chemical company anticipated the Marihuana Tax Act in its 1937 annual report, which worried that taxes "may be converted into an instrument for forcing acceptance of sudden new ideas of industrial and social reorganization." It's far more likely that this was merely typical 1930s corporate-class complaining about the New Deal's social programs and business regulations.

Herer also claims that Pittsburgh banker Andrew Mellon—Anslinger's wife's uncle and, as Treasury Secretary, his boss from 1930 to 1932—was part of the plot, as DuPont's "chief financial backer." However, historians find no evidence of DuPont–Mellon ties. As the leading Allied manufacturer of explosives during World War I, DuPont was wealthy enough on its own.

In a country that was puritanical enough in 1919 to prohibit alcohol, the most pervasive recreational drug in the Western world, and prejudiced enough to aim its immigration restrictions at Jews and Italians and its opium laws against the Chinese, it was easy in 1937 to outlaw an unknown substance that was used

🌿 *New York Mayor Fiorello LaGuardia, whose 1944 commission on marijuana debunked prohibitionist horror stories.*

mainly by the even more despised Mexican immigrants and Afro-Americans.

In 1944, a study commissioned by New York Mayor Fiorello La Guardia concluded that the publicity about marijuana's "catastrophic effects" was "unfounded"; that pot wasn't addictive, didn't lead to heroin, didn't cause crime, and wasn't being sold to teenagers. That didn't faze Anslinger, who in the 1950s claimed that pot caused apathy and did lead to heroin. Federal laws were toughened in the 1950s.

Anslinger's final legacy was the 1961 United Nations Single Convention on Narcotic Drugs, a treaty that required signatories to ban the sale and cultivation of marijuana. It remains a key obstacle to legalization. The convention also vowed to eradicate the nonmedical use of cannabis within 25 years.

## If You're a Viper: Jazz and Reefer

Pot-smoking as a tradition among musicians began with the jazz players of the 1920s and 1930s, when smoke hissing through the lips of "vipers" accompanied the sound of boogie pianos and drums and horns cutting loose. "If we all get as old as Methuselah our memories will always be of lots of beauty and warmth from gage," Louis Armstrong told biographer Max Jones.

Armstrong's 1928 instrumental "Muggles" was among the first of a spate of reefer songs, including Ella Fitzgerald's "When I Get Low, I Get High," Benny Goodman's "Texas Tea Party," and the oft-recorded anthem of Jazz Age stoners, "If You're a Viper."

> Dreamed about a reefer five feet long
> The mighty mezz but not too strong
> You'll be high but not for long
> If you're a viper

The "mighty mezz" referred to the joints sold by Mezz Mezzrow, a clarinetist who worked with Armstrong and Sidney Bechet. "Tea puts a musician in a real masterly sphere," wrote Mezzrow. "You hear everything at once and you hear it right." Even Harry Anslinger believed that marijuana made jazz musicians able to play more notes. That didn't stop him from keeping dossiers on suspected "weed hounds," including Armstrong, Duke Ellington, and Dizzy Gillespie. Armstrong, jailed in 1931 for getting high in the parking lot of a Los Angeles club, was the first celebrity pot bust.

The reefer songs faded after prohibition—"The G-Man got the tea man," one would lament in 1945—but jazz musicians kept on puffing. "In every band, at least half the musicians smoked reefers," Malcolm X wrote in his autobiography. As a teenage Harlem hustler in the early 1940s, Malcolm financed following bands around the country by dealing to them.

"I had Big Apple reefers," he explained. "Nobody had ever heard of a traveling reefer peddler."

🌿 Duke Ellington (far left): His musicians recorded "Sweet Marihuana Brown." Louis Armstrong (left): A devout viper.

# THE 1960S
# EIGHT MILES HIGH

Cannabis was a crucial component in the mass bohemianism of the 1960s. Weed became widespread, filtered through the cultural and political rebellions of the era, the manifestations of what hippie-radical poet John Sinclair called "total assault on the culture"—Jimi Hendrix's lysergic synesthesia of blues, funky flash, and amplified anarchy, French anarchists proclaiming "Be realistic—demand the impossible," and drag queens battling police in New York's 1969 Stonewall riots.

The beginnings were with a group of writers later known as the Beats, who quietly defied the communist-phobic, rigidly heterosexual culture of 1950s America, in which "dope" meant every depraved demon in Harry Anslinger's bestiary. The likes of Jack Kerouac, Allen Ginsberg, and Lawrence Ferlinghetti were proud weed-smokers, using it to stimulate spontaneous, jazz-style "bop prosody" like Kerouac's *Mexico City Blues*.

Ginsberg and other post-Beat literati—Sinclair in Detroit, d.a. levy in Cleveland, and Michael Aldrich in Buffalo, N.Y.—were the backbone of LeMar, the first pot-legalization group in the US, founded in 1964. In 1965's "First Manifesto to End the Bringdown," Ginsberg denounced marijuana prohibition as "barbarous" and "mass brainwashing," contrasting Moroccan kif-smokers' "model of tranquil sensibility" with the TV imagery of "drunken American violence covering the world." He posited pot as a catalyst for a "new consciousness," a revived holy primitivism to cope with the complexity and destructiveness of modern civilization, with African religious rites transmuted into jazz and rock'n'roll.

As the jazz scene had done in the 1930s, rock culture spread grass to the masses in the 1960s. Bob Dylan got the Beatles high for the first time in 1964, and the effects were soon obvious in the more nuanced, complex music of their 1965

🌿 *Jack Kerouac: "Starspangled Kingdoms bedecked in dewy joint."*

*Rubber Soul* album. As the baby boom's hedonistic youth culture of rock'n'roll and surfing merged with the Beats' ecstatic-dropout philosophy and the idealism of the civil rights and peace movements, a new hippie subculture emerged, and pot and LSD were its vessels of "consciousness expansion." Thinly coded drug songs slipped into the Top 40—the Byrds' "Eight Miles High," the Jefferson Airplane's "White Rabbit," and Dylan's "Rainy Day Women #12 and #35," with its woozy, nasal chorus of "everybody must get stoned."

By 1967, the hippie culture had full-blown enclaves in San Francisco's Haight-Ashbury district, New York's Lower East Side, and London's Notting Hill. European hippies interested in Eastern religion trekked to India and Nepal, finding *charas* and the hashish shops of Katmandu.

1968 was the year of apocalypse. On March 31, with the Vietnam war a bloody stalemate and the peace movement growing, President Lyndon B. Johnson announced that he wouldn't seek re-election. Five days later, Martin Luther King was assassinated, shattering the dream of nonviolent civil rights, and black neighborhoods erupted in riots. A near-revolution burst in France in May, with a melange of radical students, anarchist ideologues, and union members almost toppling the government. In August, the Soviet Union invaded Czechoslovakia,

crushing both the Prague government's "socialism with a human face" and the fledgling Czech counterculture. A week later, Chicago police battered hippie-radical demonstrators at the Democratic Convention on national TV. On October 2 in Mexico City, the army massacred hundreds of protesters during the Olympic Games.

The net result of all this in the United States was a bitter cultural war. Richard Nixon, elected president in November 1968, symbolized the "unyoung, unpoor, unblack" side; more crudely put, the side that hated "commie-fag dopers," "women's libbers," and what Nixon would call "[ethnic characterization deleted]."

*A predawn raid in 1968 nabbed pot-smoking students in Stony Brook, N.Y.*

*Bob Dylan, who turned the Beatles on to pot, mysteriously posing with a Fender Jazz Bass.*

🌿 *John Lennon: His pot bust and radical politics almost got him deported from the United States.*

🌿 *Jimi Hendrix: "Purple haze is in my brain."*

people for possessing marijuana and LSD. A year later, two Stony Brook professors were jailed for 10 days for contempt of court when they refused to answer a county prosecutor's questions about whether specific students used drugs.

Federal Bureau of Investigation director J. Edgar Hoover, whose secret COINTELPRO program worked to sabotage the antiwar and civil-rights movements, urged his underlings to nail pot-smoking leftists. In Michigan, John Sinclair, manager of the MC5, the only band to play the 1968 Chicago protests, got nine years in prison in 1969 for giving two joints to an undercover cop. Texas black activist Lee Otis Johnson got 30 years for passing a joint—technically "sale"—in 1968. (Both were released in the early 1970s.)

Not everyone getting high was against the war. Soldiers in Vietnam discovered the extremely potent local weed. Dennis Peron, a draftee who launched his career as San Francisco's most brazen dealer with two pounds of Vietnamese in 1970, was just one of many veterans who brought reefer home, an important factor in spreading pot in the South and rural America. When the Army cracked down in 1968, thousands of GIs turned instead to the extremely cheap local heroin.

In October 1969, Nixon launched Operation Intercept to stop the marijuana trade from Mexico, ordering guards at the

Pot was an obvious target. In 1968, there were 50,000 marijuana arrests in California, most for petty quantities. At 5 a.m. on January 17, 1968, almost 200 cops raided the dormitories at the State University of New York at Stony Brook—where the dean estimated that one third of students smoked pot—and arrested 35

border to search every vehicle. It caused monumental traffic jams that crippled trade, forced smugglers to turn professional to survive, and created a pot shortage that encouraged users to turn to other drugs. As the broken idealism of the counterculture crumbled into rage and despair, its taboo against heroin eroded, particularly at the extremes of rock-star riches and strung-out street-hippie poverty. "'Consciousness Expansion' went out with LBJ... and it is worth noting, historically, that downers came in with Nixon," Hunter S. Thompson wrote in *Fear and Loathing in Las Vegas*.

The end of the decade saw the escalation of the war on cannabis codified in law. In 1969, the Supreme Court held the 1937 Marihuana Tax Act unconstitutional, on the grounds that LSD advocate Timothy Leary, busted at the

## Pop Stars Popped for Possession

Among the rock musicians popped for possession were John Lennon and George Harrison of the Beatles, the Grateful Dead, and Brian Jones and Keith Richards of the Rolling Stones. Richards, given a year in prison in 1967 for letting people smoke cannabis in his house, got off on appeal after *The Times* of London criticized his sentence in an editorial entitled "Who Breaks a Butterfly on a Wheel?" Charles Neville of New Orleans' legendary Neville Brothers served three years in Louisiana's notorious Angola prison for two joints. Roky Erickson, lead singer of the Austin Texas, psychedelic-garage band the 13th Floor Elevators, probably got it worst: Arrested for possession of about a joint in 1967, he spent three years in a prison for the criminally insane.

Texas border with three ounces in 1965, would have been incriminating himself under state law if he'd paid the tax. The Nixon administration responded with the Controlled Substances Act of 1970, which banned pot outright and declared it had "no valid medical use." France and Britain enacted similar laws in 1970 and 1971.

🌿 *Washington burns after the murder of Dr. Martin Luther King Jr. in April 1968.*

# THE 1970S
# MASS-MARKET MARIJUANA

In the 1970s, marijuana moved from being a bohemian and ghetto drug to a mass-market product. Bob Dylan may have sang "everybody must get stoned" in the 1960s, but pot use became much more common in the 1970s. It seemed like everyone, from waitresses to presidents' sons, basketball players to train conductors, was enjoying a toke. By 1978, according to one widely used survey, one-sixth of Americans over 12 got high at least once a year.

A generation grew up cleaning the seeds out of their weed on the fold-out cover of Pink Floyd's *Dark Side of the Moon*. Headshops sprouted in shopping malls, selling rolling papers and pipes—from small plumbing-part brass pipes to towering bongs in blood-red plastic—along with T-shirts ("Smoke the Best—Smoke Colombian") and posters (Day-Glo depictions of sex positions, one for each sign of the zodiac). Stoner comedians Cheech and Chong advertised their *Up in Smoke* film with the slogan "Don't come straight to see this movie." *High Times*, the magazine for pot-smokers, began publication in 1974 and within three years was selling over 500,000 copies a month.

Such a large market required a massive and consistent supply. If many 1960s smugglers had been amateurs, Haight-Ashbury hippies and Southern California surfers making weekend trips to Mexico to bring back a few kilo bricks, importation became professional in the 1970s, with sophisticated operations bringing in multi-ton loads in planes and boats. "There are two kinds of dealers—those who need a forklift and those who don't," bragged Tom Forçade, the mercurial

*Michigan stoners light up at the 1973 Hash Bash in Ann Arbor. The city lowered its penalty for pot possession to a $5 fine in 1972.*

smuggler/journalist who founded *High Times* and committed suicide in 1978.

Colombia and Jamaica, which grew pot noticeably more potent than Mexican, emerged as new sources. This caused prices to rise, but most US tokers were willing to pay $40 for an ounce of good commercial Colombian rather than $15 for a lid of dubious weed soaked in Coca-Cola to increase its weight. The 1970s also saw the beginning of the connoisseur market, with Thai sticks, Colombian Santa Marta Gold, and Mexican and domestic sinsemilla commanding premium prices. And the first seeds of home-growing were planted, by back-to-the-land hippies in California and the Northwest and bootleggers' grandsons in the Southeast.

One method of smuggling was the "mothership," in which a large vessel bearing several tons of cannabis would anchor off the coast, usually South Florida, and the crew transfer its cargo to smaller speedboats.

This meant that if one of the smaller boats got caught or had to dump its stuff, most of the load would still get through. Other smugglers flew rickety old propeller planes, DC-3s or P-38s, from primitive airstrips hidden in Colombia's Guajira peninsula. Legendary British importer Howard Marks used the mothership method to bring 15 tons from Colombia to Scotland, and shipped half-ton loads of hashish from Europe to the US hidden in speaker cabinets for imaginary rock bands.

With the rising number of potheads, many with respectable, middle-class careers, the push for legalization grew. NORML, the National Organization for the Reform of Marijuana Laws, was founded in 1970. In Canada, the Le Dain Commission recommended lowering the punishment for pot possession to a $100 fine. In 1972, the Shafer Commission, appointed by President Richard Nixon to study the marijuana laws,

*Richard Nixon, father of the "War on Drugs." "Every one of the bastards that are out for legalizing marijuana is Jewish," Nixon told his chief of staff in 1971.*

🌿 *The many faces of master smuggler Howard Marks. Marks, Britain's biggest hashish importer in the 1970s and 1980s, also had several aliases.*

concluded that the laws did more harm to users and society than the drug did. Nixon, who thought that legalizing pot was a Jewish plot, ignored its recommendations, but from 1974 to 1977, 11 states, including New York and California, "decriminalized" marijuana, reducing penalties for possession of small quantities to the level of a stiff traffic-ticket fine.

Pot was smoked openly in many places, especially rock concerts, and the mood among stoners was that it was going to be legal soon, especially as pot-smoking law students moved into politics. In 1975, Alaska's highest court ruled the state's law against marijuana possession unconstitutional, saying it violated the right

to privacy. President Jimmy Carter endorsed decriminalization in a 1977 speech.

A similar process was occurring in the Netherlands, where the first hashish shop opened in 1972. The government there decriminalized cannabis in 1976, leaving people with less than five grams (about ⅙ oz) alone as long as they weren't too obnoxious. Jamaica eliminated the 18-month mandatory sentence for possession, which had ensnared reggae luminaries Bunny Wailer and Toots Hibbert.

Still, marijuana arrests in the US, less than 120,000 in 1969, topped 400,000 every year from 1973 through 1978. By late in the decade, a backlash was brewing. As smuggling and dealing became a

multimillion-dollar enterprise, it soured for the once-counterculture, never-use-a-gun types who had gotten into it for the love of unlimited smoke and easy money. More conventional criminals moved in, and "the results were predictable," as Howard Marks wrote in his autobiography, *Mr. Nice*: "A lot more ruthlessness and violence." Allen Long, who imported more than a million pounds over the decade, went from dealing to Michigan academic hippies to partnerships with South Florida Cuban-exile gangsters, who'd cut him out of his share on a load and then threaten to kill him for ripping *them* off. Getting involved in outlaw business could be fatal for the naïve; there were several stories of young dealers going to Arizona, where pot that fetched $40 an ounce in the Northeast wholesaled for under $85 a pound, and disappearing after being invited to the desert "to see the stash." Cocaine became pervasive in the "hipoisie," the cannabis world's upper classes.

Despite Carter's verbal support for decriminalization, his administration was supplying the Mexican government with paraquat, a lethal, lung-destroying herbicide, to spray marijuana fields. Little, if any, tainted pot reached the US market, but potheads were enraged and terrified. In 1978, when Peter Bourne, Carter's decrim-friendly drug-policy adviser, was accused of snorting cocaine at a NORML party, NORML officials failed to protect him. Bourne resigned, and the doors to the White House closed to the legalization movement. For the next 23 years, no states decriminalized pot.

As the age of pot use dropped, with children as young as 12 and 13 smoking weed and a 1978 survey reporting that 10 percent of high-school seniors got high every day, irate parents began to organize anti-pot campaigns, concentrating on headshops. Drug-paraphernalia laws enacted in 1979–80 crippled the headshop business.

*Rock festivals, like this one on Britain's Isle of Wight in 1970, showed how massive the 1960s counterculture had become—and that it could become a mass market.*

# A STALK OF SINSEMILLA
# GANJA AND REGGAE

**If you've ever used the expressions "herb" or "spliff," you're showing reggae's cultural influence. No other art form is as intertwined with cannabis.**

Be it Bob Marley's "Kaya," Black Uhuru's "Sinsemilla," or Linval Thompson's "I Love Marijuana," its indelible image is a dreadlocked Rastaman exhaling a huge cloud of smoke as he croons a paean to Jah herb over a sinuous, pulsing bass-and-drums riddim. "When mi smoke up de mariguana, it give mi a vibes, a powerful vibes," said Thompson. Most Jamaicans are not spliff-puffing dreads—Rastafarians form a small minority of the country's 2.6 million residents—but ganja use is "culturally entrenched," says anthropologist Barry Chevannes. It was widespread enough for the British colonial government to prohibit it in 1913, and recent surveys indicate that almost half of men and about one-sixth of women over 15 have gotten high at least once.

Rastafarianism began in 1930s as sort of black Zionism, mixing Old Testament exile longing with Marcus Garvey's visions of repatriation to Africa. It adopted herb, the "wisdom weed" of Jamaican spiritual seekers, as a sacrament, finding backing in the Bible from Genesis ("Behold, I have given you every herb bearing seed") to Revelation ("and the leaves of the tree were for the healing of the nations").

Though scorned by many Jamaicans, both ganja and Rasta found a niche in the country's expanding record industry in the late '60s. Studio One, reggae's birthplace, was popular among musicians because "you could smoke weed there," as singer

🌿 *A Rastafarian man holds his chicken as he smokes a spliff. Was he listening to Lee Perry's "Kentucky Skank"?*

Horace Andy told *This Is Reggae Music* author Lloyd Bradley. "People want to come there because they know that would make the right vibe for the music." By the mid-1970s, Rasta themes were pervasive. Peter Tosh's "Legalize It" hit #1 in Jamaica in 1975. (Tosh recorded the song three years after police beat him unconscious during a ganja bust.)

The herbal influence showed in the sound as much as in the lyrics. Perhaps the stoniest of all music genres is dub, the instrumental-remix versions of reggae records developed for sound-system dances in the late 1960s. With the song stripped down to the riddim and cryptic, echo-drenched fragments of the vocal, the bass powerful and viscous, and the drums magnified to eerie, cosmic intensity, you can almost smell the spliff leaking out of the speakers.

Rastafarianism's ascendance in reggae coincided with the music's arrival in Europe and the United States—long hair, pot, and denouncing the "shitstem," sound familiar? The 1972 film *The Harder They Come* starred Jimmy Cliff as a fugitive ganja dealer and outlaw hero. Bob Marley and the Wailers began cutting records aimed at the international market. Jamaican immigrants in Britain provided enough of a fan base for reggae for punk-rockers to pick up on it.

In the 1980s, Jamaican audiences largely turned to the blatantly sexual, prerecorded-riddim styles of dancehall reggae, but the herb songs have kept on coming, from Wayne Smith's all-electronic "Under Mi Sleng Teng" in 1985 to Sister Carol's "Red Eye" in 1996 to Jr. Kelly's "Boom Draw" in 2001. An obscure DJ named Ranking Dread perhaps best summed up reggae culture's attitude when he cut a version of Linval Thompson's song: "Oh God, I love marijuana."

*Bob Marley: "Excuse me while I light my spliff."*

# THE 1980S
# REPRESSION AND REGENERATION

The 1980s were a harsh time for marijuana-smokers. "A conservative cultural revolution took place. It was called the Drug War," exulted John Walters, a top drug-policy official under President George Bush I. President Ronald Reagan's far-right administration declared war on the legacy of the 1960s, on gay rights, antiwar attitudes, and ganja.

Spearheaded by future New York Mayor Rudolph Giuliani, it concentrated its drug policy on eradicating marijuana. CAMP, the Campaign Against Marijuana Planting, sent heavily armed police into the "emerald triangle" of northern California, buzzing peoples' homes in helicopters and smashing through suspected pot-growers' doors. In Jamaica, the US-backed conservative government elected in 1980—after an extraordinarily bloody campaign—sent soldiers to burn ganja fields. Sea patrols choked off the smuggling lanes of the Caribbean.

The net result of this was that the Colombian drug trade turned to cocaine, which was far easier to smuggle and much more profitable than pot. When crack, smokable cocaine, exploded into big-city ghettoes in 1985–86, it set off a new round of militarized policing and tougher laws. Mandatory minimum sentencing meant that pot-growers got an automatic five years in prison for 100 plants, and expanded forfeiture procedures let police confiscate a car or a house if a single joint was found in it.

Pot got lumped in with crack and heroin as "illegal drugs." "Just Say No" was the mantra of Reagan's wife, Nancy, and those who said yes were tarred as lowlife scum, abetting the gangs killing each other for

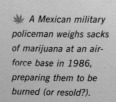
🌿 *A Mexican military policeman weighs sacks of marijuana at an air-force base in 1986, preparing them to be burned (or resold?).*

🍁 *The notorious black helicopters, searching the countryside for marijuana.*

it gave people the idea that they could use "drugs" without destroying their lives.

Two bright spots appeared during the decade. With supplies of Jamaican and Colombian pot decimated, domestic growing expanded to take its place. Farmers in the rainy Pacific Northwest traveled to Afghanistan to bring back cannabis indica seeds, strains more suited for growing without tropical sunshine. And the Netherlands sprouted coffeeshops, quasi-legal cannabis bars. Growers there began using hydroponic techniques to cultivate herb for the coffeeshops.

control of the new crack trade. Drug testing, which detected marijuana far more easily than it did cocaine or heroin, became widespread. Ronald Reagan proudly peed into a jar to demonstrate his devotion to the cause.

In 1989, the Drug Enforcement Administration tried to shut down marijuana magazines with "Operation Green Merchant," raiding the garden-supply shops that advertised in them and tracking down their customers. *High Times* survived, but *Sinsemilla Tips* didn't. US drug czar William Bennett, a self-righteous moralist (later author of *The Book of Virtues*) and compulsive gambler, argued that occasional pot use was more destructive than crack addiction, because

By the mid-1980s, growers in the US, Canada, and the Netherlands were swapping seeds and beginning to develop myriad new strains. Grass-roots supply was culturally healthier than the big-money excesses of 1970s smuggling. But the combination of improved quality and heavy repression meant that prices zoomed dramatically. In 1980, $40 or $50 could buy an ounce of pot in the Northeast. By 1990, it was barely enough for a quarter—and soon would get only an eighth.

# THE DUTCH COFFEESHOP CULTURE

The cannabis coffeeshops of the Netherlands, into which any adult can walk and order marijuana or hashish off the menu like ordering a drink in a bar, are unique in the world. Sales of up to five grams to a customer are officially tolerated, and today the country has about 800 coffeeshops, catering to tourists and locals, serving myriad varieties of pot and "hasj" to soundtracks of techno, reggae, and classic rock.

Among them are the Greenhouse, Global Chillage, and Lucky Mothers in Amsterdam, the Sensi Smile Cafe in Rotterdam, and the Willie Wortel chain in Haarlem. They also sell food, such as "tostis," grilled sandwiches, and often have a pool table or table-soccer game.

Amsterdam's cannabis scene grew out of its 1960s counterculture, in which a group called the Provos proposed that the city buy thousands of white bicycles so anyone could ride for free. In 1969, two former Provos, Kees Hoekert and Robert Jasper Grootveld, founded the Lowlands Weed Company, selling 30,000 plants for a guilder (about 35 cents) apiece from their houseboat.

Invaded by a quarter-million hippie tourists a year in the early 1970s, the Netherlands applied its tradition of pragmatic social libertarianism to cannabis. Amsterdam tolerated open hash-smoking in the Vondelpark, its main park, and ran a $1-a-night hostel with an unofficial house dealer. Hippie clubs and community centers like the Melkweg and the Paradiso had signs reading "Roken Ja—Dealing Nee" (Smoking Yes—Dealing No).

The first coffeeshop, Mellow Yellow, opened in 1972 in a vacant bakery squatted by Wernard Bruining and friends, and painted to look like a yellow submarine with portholes. It was followed by Rusland in 1974 and the Bulldog, a converted sex shop in the red-light district, in 1975. These established the "no hard drugs, no violence" principles of coffeeshop operation.

The Dutch government decriminalized cannabis in 1976. With heroin use rising, they decided that tolerating coffeeshops and not prosecuting possession of less than 30 grams would separate the markets for soft and hard drugs.

❧ OPPOSITE *Amsterdam's Smokey coffeeshop, one of about 800 places where you can legally buy and smoke cannabis.*

🌿 *Where can you find a coffeeshop? These maps, guides, and business cards might help.*

At first, the coffeeshops sold mostly imported hashish, but they evolved toward marijuana as local cultivation developed in the 1980s. Bruining hooked up with an American refugee grower named Old Ed to cultivate a crop of sinsemilla in 1980, and founded the Lowlands Seed Company, the first seed company, with Kees Hoekert. By 1995, Dutch-grown "Nederwiet" was outselling hash.

Regulations remained uncertain until the early 1990s, when the government announced its "AHOJG" policy: no advertising, no hard drugs, no disturbing the peace, and no more than 500 grams on the premises. The rules also raised the smoking age from 16 to 18—which caused Willie Wortel owner Nol van Schaik to collect petitions from parents, protesting that this would expose their children to hard-drugs dealers. Growing remains illegal, but police usually overlook the "back door" supply. "Tolerance at the back door is what keeps the system working," a Haarlem police official told *Travel and Leisure* magazine in 2000.

The cannabis-tolerance policy appears to have worked. Most Netherlands heroin users now are over 35, and Dutch teenagers smoke cannabis less than their British or American counterparts—though, like the rest of Western Europe, there is a widespread Ecstasy-taking rave culture. However, the Dutch government is moving to crack down on cultivation and reduce the number of coffeeshops, especially in border towns where they draw mainly French and German "drug tourists."

# POT IN THE PRESENT

Cannabis occupies an odd position in today's world. Millions of people smoke it all over the planet, but there's no common subculture. Much of Western Europe and some Latin American countries have decriminalized it, but there is no nation where it can be grown and sold as legally as liquor.

In the United States, its use is widely acknowledged, but heavily repressed; pot-theme T-shirts ("MariJuana: Over 1 Billion Stoned") are sold wherever tourists congregate, but there have been record numbers of arrests since the late 1990s. A substantial number of politicians admit to having "experimented" with it, but virtually none will say that other people should be allowed to use it legally.

After the prohibitionist mania of the 1980s, pot re-entered the mainstream in the early 1990s. Top-selling hip-hop records celebrated it; some people argue that the decline in crime in the 1990s came from ghetto youth becoming disgusted with the crack trade's carnage and turning to blunts and malt liquor instead. Bill Clinton, the first presidential candidate born after World War II, caused a stir in the 1992 campaign when he confessed that he had used marijuana, but "didn't inhale."

The movement against prohibition revived in the 1990s. Voters in eight states passed laws legalizing medical marijuana, most prominently California in 1996. Nevada, the last state where marijuana possession was an automatic felony, decriminalized it in 2001. However, the state's voters rejected an initiative to legalize possession of up to three ounces in 2002.

As the escalated war on drugs continued, its excesses became painfully obvious. In the Los Angeles suburbs, millionaire rancher Donald Scott was shot to death in 1992 by police looking for nonexistent pot plants—they coveted seizing his mountaintop land under forfeiture. In Oklahoma, Will Foster, an arthritic father of three, got 93 years in prison in 1997 for growing about 70 plants and seedlings in his basement. Prison populations multiplied, passing two million by 2000. In some states, more than 90 percent of the people incarcerated for drugs were black or Latino, and more African-American men were in prison than in college. "Racial profiling" and "driving while black" emerged as major issues.

The 1999 raids in the small town of Tulia, Texas, though not involving marijuana, graphically illustrated the racism of the war on drugs: 46 people, almost all African-American, were charged with selling small amounts of cocaine, and several got prison sentences of over 60 years. Most were freed after one defendant proved she'd been in Oklahoma, 300 miles away, at the time of the alleged sale. The undercover officer who'd set up the busts had been fired from his previous police job for fraud.

None of this did much to reduce pot-smoking. As prices rose—top-quality bud can cost $500 an ounce—home-growing boomed, aided by the proliferation of seed companies and improved hydroponic and lighting technology.

Outside the United States, marijuana laws are being relaxed—officially or unofficially—in several countries. In Western Europe, where cannabis became a common youth-culture drug in the 1990s, Spain and Switzerland have widespread and open pot-growing, while Britain, Belgium, Portugal, and Italy have all eased their laws. Colombia, ravaged by cocaine wars, has legalized possession of up to 20 grams.

In Canada, where laws were once strict enough that literature deemed to encourage illegal drug use or production was forbidden until 1994, several court decisions have said the government cannot ban medical marijuana or arrest people for possession. Vancouver has several cafes where pot is smoked or cooked—though not sold—openly.

Canada, especially British Columbia, emerged as an exporter in the late 1990s. Still, in many parts of the United States, people are smoking Mexican, which sells for as low as $40 an ounce in Texas. Today, the United States essentially has a three-tier marijuana market, with homegrown kind-bud strains at the top; Canadian, mostly B.C., imports in the middle; and Mexican the prole smoke. Compared to beer, the equivalents are microbreweries, Heineken, and Budweiser.

*Residents of Tulia, Texas, march on the state capitol in 2000 to protest racist drug frame-ups in their town. Commenting on then-governor George W. Bush's alleged cocaine use, one man observed, "He can be forgiven for a boyhood infatuation, but if our children do it, it's a hundred-year incarceration."*

The United States government remains militantly hardline. It is relatively safe to be a discreet, white, middle-class toker, but growers, activists, and younger and darker-skinned street smokers are very vulnerable. Michigan hippies Tom Crosslin and Rolland Rohm, who had enraged the local prosecutor by holding "Hemp Aid" and "Roach Roast" festivals at their Rainbow Farm campground, were killed in a confrontation with state police and FBI agents in 2001.

Comedian Lenny Bruce's 1960s joke that "pot will be legal in ten years, because every other one of you knows a law student who smokes pot, who will become a senator" proved false in the 1990s. Supreme Court Justice Clarence Thomas, once a pot-smoking law student at Yale, wrote the 2001 decision against

medical marijuana. Didn't-Inhale Clinton fired Surgeon General Dr. Joycelyn Elders in 1994 for suggesting that legalization (and masturbation) be discussed, and signed the Higher Education Act of 1998, banning federal financial aid for students convicted of drug offenses. His Republican foe, House Speaker Newt Gingrich, who said that getting high was a sign that he "was alive in graduate school," proposed the death penalty for pot smugglers.

By the late 1990s, there were 700,000 marijuana arrests a year in the United States, more than 85 percent for possession. One-tenth of those came in New York City, where fiercely authoritarian Mayor Rudolph Giuliani made public pot-smoking a top priority for police as part of his "quality of life" crusade. (He also revived a Prohibition-era law banning dancing in bars.) In 2000, pot busts in the city averaged almost 200 a day, and 80 percent of those nabbed were black or Latino. The campaign turned tragic that March, when an undercover cop outside a Midtown bar asked off-duty security guard Patrick Dorismond if he had any weed to sell. "Get the fuck out of here," Dorismond snapped. He was shot to death in the ensuing scuffle.

The 2000 presidential campaign pitted Vice President Al Gore, a regular stoner as a military journalist in Vietnam and a young newspaper reporter in Tennessee,

🌿 *Once-tolerant New York City led the nation in pot busts in 2000.*

against Texas Governor George W. Bush, a convicted drunk driver who repeatedly ducked questions about his past cocaine use. Gore came out against legalizing medical marijuana, and Bush, selected president by the Supreme Court, pursued viciously hardline drug policies.

Federal agents raided medical-marijuana growers in California, prosecuting them for as few as 20 plants. In early 2003, nationwide arrests shut down dozens of pipe manufacturers and retailers; pot comedian Tommy Chong, 65, got nine months in jail for selling glass bongs on the Internet. The US also threatened economic sanctions against Canada and Jamaica if they eased their laws.

George Bush's drug czar, fanatical prohibitionist John Walters, claimed that B.C. bud was so potent that dealers were trading ounces of it for ounces of cocaine. He could have been right. After 30 years of escalating "tough on drugs" policies, the cost of cocaine had fallen by two thirds, while pot prices increased tenfold.

Who knows what the future will bring, but as Jamaican-American novelist Michael Thelwell wrote in *The Harder They Come*, "de herb is fe evah.... Mek dem bu'n de field dem— little rain fall an' de herb spring up back, green and lovely."

## Blazing Hip-Hop

The New York City ghettoes where hip-hop was born in the 1970s were a heavily weeded world. "Pot stores," ill-disguised groceries, sold $5 and $10 bags of smoke from behind bulletproof glass. Street dealers cried, "Loose joints, six for five, try before you buy," and DJs in discos and streetlight-wired sound systems boomed funk jams like B.T. Express's "Peace Pipe" and the Harlem Underground Band's "Smokin' Cheeba Cheeba." Still, there were few rap songs with overt references to pot.

That changed in the early 1990s, with the release of three seminal albums from Southern California. They introduced the blunt—a joint rolled in a cigar leaf—to the world, and made blazing through forests of hydroponic trees a badge of hip-hop outlaw hedonism. Cypress Hill's first album, released in 1991, featured titles like "Stoned Is the Way of the Walk," "Light Another," and "Something for the Blunted." They appeared on a landmark *High Times* cover in early 1992 (giving instructions on how to roll a blunt in the centerfold) and proclaimed themselves the official rap group of NORML. Later albums included tracks named "Hits From the Bong," "Spark Another Owl," and "Dr. Greenthumb."

For 1992's *The Chronic*, Dr. Dre, formerly a member of gangsta-rap originators N.W.A., sampled a Parliament-Funkadelic classic for the title track, changing the lyrics to "Make my shit the chronic/I want to get fucked up." Bitches-ain't-shit sexist, it sold over three million copies, as did *Doggystyle*, the 1993 debut of Dre protégé Snoop Doggy Dogg. Over Dre-created soundscapes that evoked hustlers cruising the boulevards of Los Angeles' ghetto suburbs, mellow and menacing with a whining synthesizer on top, Snoop told cold-blooded tales of gangster life, "rolling down the street, smokin' indo."

Scores of reefer raps followed. Among them were Channel Live's "Mad Izm" ("Woke up this morning with the yearning for herb/Which loosens up the nouns, metaphors, and verbs"), Gang Starr's "Take Two and Pass," and the Outkast/Ludacris collaboration "Tomb of the Boom," which rhymes "dro," "hos," and "pistachios."

Snoop Doggy Dogg and Dr. Dre

Cypress Hill

# BOTANICAL FACTS

*"There are times when these migraines come on, I wish I had a gun. It's like a hot ice pick is grinding around in my brain. When I smoke pot, at least it doesn't feel like my head's going to blow up."*

Marcy Duda, medical-marijuana activist, 2003

**CANNABIS** is an angiosperm, a flowering plant, a category of flora that first developed during the Cretaceous era. It's dioecious, which means that it has two sexes, and distinctive, containing an entire class of chemicals not found in any other plant. Probably native to central Asia, it has been cultivated by humans for at least 5,000 years, at first for hemp fiber and later for its intoxicating and medicinal effects. The plant produces the psychoactive chemical tetrahydrocannabinol (THC), concentrated most strongly in the flowers of the female.

Until relatively recently, almost all the intoxicating varieties of the plant grew in the tropical latitudes. Cultivation in the United States, Canada, and Europe was for hemp, and wild cannabis—the roadside "ditchweed" of Kentucky—was the legacy of hemp production. The late 20th century saw a revolution in cannabis breeding and cultivation, as illicit growers crossed plants from all over the world and developed agronomic techniques to produce the most potent, lushest, and fastest-growing plants possible under clandestine-garden conditions, especially indoors.

# ANATOMY OF A CANNABIS PLANT

"From the root to the Rizla," from the first white sprouts emerging from the seeds to the THC-rich trichome glands that frost top-quality buds, the cannabis plant's anatomy—and the way growers manipulate its quirks—determines its destiny.

## THE SEEDLING

🌿 The first stage of the plant's life.

**TAPROOT** The plant's main root, sprouted from the seed.

**HYPOCOTYL** First part of the stem to appear above ground.

**COTYLEDONS** The first leaves the seedling grows, two small ovals.

**FIRST TRUE LEAVES** The second pair of leaves are the first to have serrated edges, and usually have only one blade.

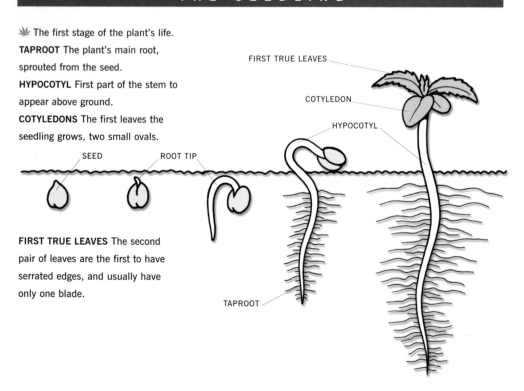

FIRST TRUE LEAVES

COTYLEDON

HYPOCOTYL

SEED

ROOT TIP

TAPROOT

# THE MALE PLANT

Male plants are usually taller than females. Contrary to common belief, they do contain THC—just much less than the buds of the female, especially sinsemilla buds.

**STEM** Fiber from bark is used for hemp; woody core produces "hurds."

**NODES** Places where branches grow on the main stem.

**INTERNODES** Sections of stem in between branches.

**PETIOLES** Stems of leaves.

**LEAVES** Cannabis' trademark leaves have five to seven blades, but some can go up to 11.

**FAN LEAVES** Large outermost leaves on lower branches.

**STAMINATE FLOWERS** These sacs release pollen to fertilize the female.

FLOWERS

INTERNODE

YOUNG MALE FLOWER

SEPAL

PETALS

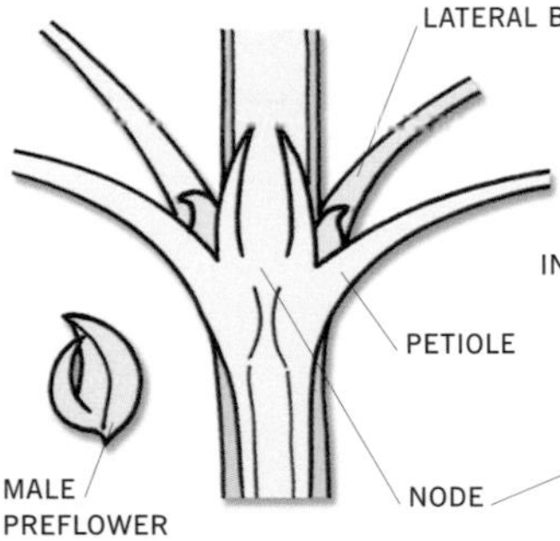

LATERAL BRANCH

INTERNODE

PETIOLE

MALE PREFLOWER

NODE

FAN LEAVES

# THE FEMALE PLANT

Females are the most prized by cannabis growers, as the flowers they produce—the buds—are the most potent part of the plant. If pollinated by the male, they produce seeds; if not, they grow the seedless buds known as sinsemilla.

**FEMALE PREFLOWER** The first sign of flowering, and a crucial early indicator of the plant's sex.

**BUDS** The clusters of flowers that sprout at the nodes, the top, and the tips of branches.

**CALYX** Pod for the young flowers. Becomes a seed pod if fertilized.

**COLA** Spanish for "tail," can be any cluster of buds, but usually means the large bud at the top of the main stem.

BUDS

COLA

PETIOLES

STIPULES

FAN LEAVES

STEM

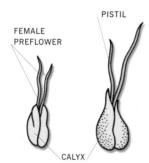

FEMALE
PREFLOWER

PISTIL

CALYX

# THE BUD

The most desirable part of the plant for smoking. Cannabis indica buds are denser and usually bigger than cannabis sativa buds, which also tend to be more spread out on the plant.

**TRIM LEAVES** Leaves growing within buds, usually having one or three blades. Most growers trim them off after harvest.

**PISTILS** Twin projections that catch pollen, usually copper-colored. Appear as red hairs on dried buds.

**TRICHOMES** These minuscule resin glands, which look like a dusting of small white crystals, contain more THC than any other part of the bud.

FLOWER

TRIM LEAVES

# PLANT PRODUCTS

The cannabis plant's products can be divided into three categories: those made from the seeds and stalks, which don't get you high; the leaves and flowers, which do get you high; and those made from the resin, the most potent.

## HEMP

Hemp refers to products made from the plant for non-psychoactive purposes, either from the seeds or fiber. These include rope, cloth, paper, and more exotic uses like flour, shampoo, and construction materials. It has a long role in history—from the Vikings to the 20th century, the ships of the world were rigged with hemp. The seeds, if guaranteed sterile, are used for bird food. Hempseed oil can be either burned for fuel or poured on salad. You can't smoke hemp and get more than a sore throat. Cannabis plants grown for fiber generally contain very little THC, the plant's main psychoactive ingredient, and are cultivated to produce mostly stalks and seeds, the parts of the plant that have the least THC. Hempseed-based food won't get you high either.

## MARIJUANA

Marijuana is the dried leaves, flowers, and buds of the plant. The leaves and the male plant contain some THC, but not a lot. What is usually sold as marijuana is the buds, the flowers of the female plant, its most potent part. They have glands that, in order to catch pollen from the male, exude sticky resin containing THC. If they are pollinated, they produce seed. If they are not pollinated, they keep producing resin and grow without seeds—"sinsemilla" in Spanish.

Marijuana is usually bright green or dark green to brown, depending on how it's dried. Some varieties have strong red, gold, or purple overtones.

*Harvesting hemp in Madagascar. The fibers are used for rope and cloth.*

*Kif* is the Moroccan word for cannabis and smoking preparations made from it. "Kif is like fire—a little warms, a lot burns," says one proverb.

## HASHISH

Hashish is produced by collecting the resin particles from the plant buds and pressing them into a block. It is usually more potent than all but the strongest marijuana, though the cheap "soap bar" Moroccan hashish sold widely in Europe is often adulterated. It can be black, golden brown, yellowish green, coppery or maroon red, or black on the outside and olive on the inside.

Historically, hashish was made in the area stretching from North Africa to the Himalayas, primarily in Morocco, Lebanon, Afghanistan, Pakistan, Nepal, and India (where it is called *charas*). Recently, hash-making has emerged in the cannabis-growing centers of the West, from "Nederhash" in Holland to "water hash" and "bubble hash," in which cannabis

plant matter is placed in ice water and the resin particles filtered out with microscopically porous "bubble bags."

## TRICHOMES

Trichomes are the stalked glands that produce the resin. They are small, about the size of pinheads, and appear as either sugary crystals on the buds or as a yellowish-white powder when collected. They are very potent.

## HASH OIL

Hash oil is a thick, sticky ooze, extracted by a complicated process of soaking cannabis in alcohol or another solvent and then distilling or evaporating the mixture. It and trichomes are the most potent cannabis products.

🌿 *Vials of hash oil, an extremely potent cannabis extract.*

# ACTIVE INGREDIENTS
# THC AND MORE

**Cannabis contains almost 500 different chemicals, including over 60 "cannabinoids"— compounds found only in this plant. These include cannabidiol (CBD), cannabinol (CBN), various cannabichromenes, cannabigerols, and cannabicyclols, and more. Other chemicals give the herb its odor.**

The main active ingredient is delta-9 tetrahydrocannabinol, $C_{21}H_{30}O_2$, a butterfly-shaped molecule known as THC. An almost identical molecule, delta-8 tetrahydrocannabinol, is less common. Delta-9 THC is metabolized in the liver, especially after oral ingestion, to 11-hydroxy delta-9 THC, which is significantly more potent and reaches the brain more easily. All cannabinoids are "lipophilic," soluble only in fatty substances but not in water, so eating cannabis with butter or other fatty foods will increase absorption of THC. THC degrades to CBN when exposed to light, heat, or air. THC was isolated from hashish in 1964 by Israeli biochemists Dr. Raphael Mechoulam and Yehiel Gaoni. Receptors for it in the brain were discovered in the early 1990s.

What the other constituents of cannabis do, and how that affects the quality of the high and the drug's medical efficacy for various syndromes, is not well known yet. Some acidic cannabinoids turn to THC when raw cannabis is cooked or smoked. As for medical use, Mechoulam wrote in 1999 that the synergism between THC and other cannabinoids "may play a role in the widely held (but not experimentally based) view that in some cases plants are better drugs than the natural products isolated from them."

CBD, which becomes THC as the plant matures, but remains in high quantities in some strains, is the second main ingredient. It may not be psychoactive

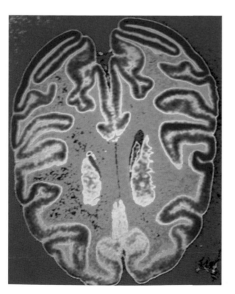

*The body transforms THC into 11-hydroxy THC before it reaches the cannabinoid receptors in the brain.*

## THC Content

The THC (tetrahydrocannabinol) content in marijuana varies widely. Less than 1% THC is hemp; 2% THC is schwag; 4%–8% is good; 10%–15% is spectacular; and over 20% is usually—though not always—grower boasting or government propaganda.

*Some early 1980s homegrown: Yes, there was plenty of potent pot around in the past.*

itself—though some research indicates sedative and anxiety-reducing effects—but it slows the metabolism of THC in the liver. Thus, CBD may intensify the high while moderating some of the negative effects, such as paranoia, and increasing sleepiness. Classic tropical sativas have high THC and little CBD, while indicas contain both THC and CBD, so CBD could be why indica strains have a reputation for "knockout" highs.

CBD and cannabichromene might also enhance THC's painkilling properties. CBN is mildly psychoactive, probably only about ⅒ as much as THC. Cannabis also contains 120 terpenes or terpenoids, the essential oils of the plant. These give the herb its odor—piney, fruity, or, most legendarily, skunky.

Much has been made of the alleged increase in THC concentration in marijuana since the 1970s, with prohibitionists contending that it makes pot a different and deadly drug, some claiming potency increases of 1,000 percent or more. While the supply of potent pot is definitely more consistent, due to improved cultivation techniques and more developed markets, there was certainly strong stuff around in the past. The low THC numbers often cited for the 1970s may be based on samples of very stale commercial pot.

In many ways, the potency debate is irrelevant. Whiskey has 10 times as much alcohol as beer—that's why people drink it by the shot instead of by the pint. Many argue that more potent pot is actually healthier, because you have to inhale less smoke to get the same high.

# A NATURAL HEALER
## MEDICAL CANNABIS

**Medicine was one of cannabis' earliest uses, and its healing properties are now being re-examined for appetite stimulation for AIDS patients, relieving the spasms from multiple sclerosis, and reducing the nausea from cancer chemotherapy. Cannabis is also used to treat chronic pain, migraines, sickle-cell anemia, glaucoma, and obscure, excruciating ailments like Ehlers-Danlos syndrome, arachnoiditis, and nail-patella syndrome.**

Used in traditional cultures for analgesia, insomnia, and childbirth, medical cannabis was introduced to the West in 1842 by Dr. William O'Shaughnessy, an Irish doctor who had observed its use in India. It was most commonly dispensed as a tincture, dissolved in alcohol. Queen Victoria's doctor prescribed tincture of cannabis for her menstrual cramps, and it was also recommended for migraines. However, doctors found it difficult to get exact doses and consistent effects, and its use declined after the late 19th century, due to the introduction of the hypodermic needle, the invention of aspirin, and Western medicine's general move from botanical drugs to pharmaceuticals. Prohibition was the final blow.

Paradoxically, medical cannabis revived within a few years after the US formally banned it in 1970. By 1990, two synthetic-cannabinoid drugs had been developed: Marinol (a.k.a. dronabinol), THC dissolved in sesame oil; and the rarely used nabilone, a THC analogue. Informal use of medical pot was also common. Marinol has been approved in the US for use against AIDS wasting syndrome and chemotherapy nausea, and it is also prescribed for migraines.

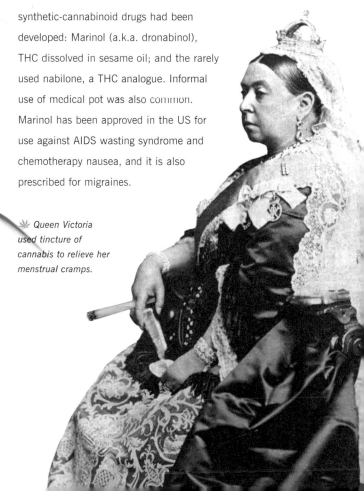

🌿 *Queen Victoria used tincture of cannabis to relieve her menstrual cramps.*

Most of the evidence for marijuana's medical efficacy comes from patients' stories. A Michigan man, run over by a truck 15 years ago, displays a 12-foot necklace of voluminous vials of Vicodin he no longer has to take. A Wisconsin woman with an agonizing joint-dislocation syndrome says pot enabled her to sit up for 90 minutes instead of 15. A San Francisco man who died of AIDS in 1996 said pot extended his life by five years. Cancer patients speak of actually wanting to eat after chemotherapy. "When I smoked marijuana, I saw more clearly," wrote glaucoma patient Robert Randall. "I'm not talking enlightenment. I'm talking sight."

These stories are called "clinical histories" by medical-marijuana supporters and dismissed as "anecdotal evidence" by its foes. Few controlled experiments have been done in the US, as the federal government, the only legal source of cannabis for research, is reluctant to allow studies that might undermine prohibition. (Another problem with "double-blind" controlled studies of smoked cannabis, in which neither the experimenter nor the subject is supposed to know who is getting the drug, is that experienced pot-smokers can almost always detect the placebo.) In Britain, a three-year study of 600 MS patients released in 2003 found little measurable difference between those taking cannabis extract and

those given a placebo, but the patients given cannabis reported sufficient improvement for the doctors to recommend approving its use.

The most ardent opposition comes from hardcore prohibitionists, who believe medical marijuana is a scam, an excuse to get high and a sneaky back door to legalization. US drug czar Barry McCaffrey dismissed it as "Cheech and Chong" medicine in 1996. Doctors tend to be more sympathetic, but wary of smoking's harmful effects and the difficulty of quantifying doses. "Take two tokes and if you feel you need more, take another" doesn't fit with a culture of "15 milligrams q.i.d."

*The Netherlands legalized medical cannabis in 2003, with plants grown under strict controls.*

🌿 *Many doctors believe marijuana has valid medical uses, but are reluctant to endorse smoking it because of the dangers of inhaling burning plant matter.*

In 1999, the federal Institute of Medicine's report, "Marijuana and Medicine: Assessing the Science Base," split the difference. It said that marijuana's components were "potentially effective," but smoking was harmful, though not "out of line" compared to other medicines' side effects. It concluded that cannabinoid compounds were preferable to plant products, but as those drugs haven't been developed yet, patients with chronic conditions could be allowed to smoke the herb "on an experimental basis."

For those opposed to smoked marijuana, the biggest problem is finding a cannabis-based medicine that is as instantly "bioavailable." Marinol, the legal alternative, must be eaten and takes one to three hours to take effect—not much good for chemotherapy patients

too nauseous to keep it down, or for migraine sufferers who need to stop an oncoming attack. It's also expensive, and shares the problems of eating marijuana—it's hard to predict whether a given dose will be enough to be effective, but not so much that it's incapacitating. In contrast, any moderately experienced pot-smoker can easily "titrate" the dose while toking.

Cannabis' psychoactive effects are most disturbing to people who have never used it. Others find that those effects are part of healing; some AIDS patients say that cannabis is the difference between "living with AIDS" and "existing with AIDS." For the terminally ill, said Valerie Corral of the Wo/Men's Alliance for Medical Marijuana in 2003, pot can be a "portal—no cure, but solace in the face of death."

Currently, medical-cannabis research is proceeding along two tracks. Some "buyers' clubs" (called "compassion clubs" in Canada) are assembling patient reports to assess which strains are most effective for various ailments. The consensus so far, says Philippe Lucas of the Vancouver Island Compassion Society in British Columbia, is that sativa strains are better for neurological conditions such as MS and epilepsy, while indicas are more effective for relieving pain. Reports by 77 patients at Corral's California club found both types equal for controlling nausea, and results have been mixed for stimulating appetite. Little is known about what might cause this; contrary to common belief, says Lucas, the indica strains used at his club did not have more CBD than the sativas.

Meanwhile, medical researchers are looking for either cannabis derivatives that have a more definable dose and don't have to be smoked, or for synthetic cannabinoid drugs that are effective without getting the patient wasted. Unless marijuana in general is legalized, it's likely that the medicinal forms allowed, at least in the US, will be either extracts or single-molecule derivatives that aren't intoxicating and can be patented by a drug company.

The British company GW Pharmaceuticals is pursuing a middle course, trying to produce standardized, consistent botanical extracts, in high-THC, high-CBD, and equal THC–CBD forms. Humans have used "complex mixtures" medically for millennia, three GW researchers argued in the *Journal of Cannabis Therapeutics* in 2001, and "in practice, it has been found that extracts of cannabis provide greater relief of pain than the equivalent amount of cannabinoid given as a single chemical entity." GW is also developing a cannabis-extract spray to be administered sublingually, under the tongue. That would be faster-acting and more controllable than eating cannabis, while safer and not much slower than smoking.

Another area of research is cannabis' "neuroprotective" effects. An endogenous (naturally occurring) cannabinoid called "anandamide" was discovered in the brain in the 1990s. In 2003, an Italian study found that CBD inhibited the growth of brain-tumor cells. There is also new research that cannabis may aid in repairing brain damage from strokes. Despite the health hazards of smoking cannabis, it is second only to injection as the fastest way to get drugs into the blood, and it remains the easiest way for the patient to control the dose. The reality, Lucas reminds us, is that "95 percent of the people using medical cannabis are smoking it."

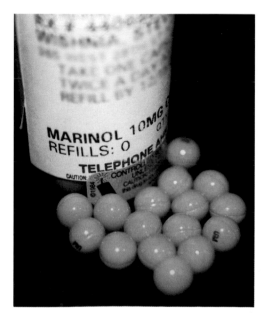

🌿 A vial of Marinol, capsules containing THC dissolved in sesame oil—the only cannabinoid drug legal in the United States.

# MARIJUANA AND MIGRAINES

Cannabis has a long history of being used to treat migraines, excruciating headaches that can last for several days and are sometimes coupled with vomiting. They affect millions of people. The cause may be a literal "brain storm," like a slow-motion epileptic seizure, with significant changes in neurotransmitters, especially serotonin.

The first use of cannabis for migraines may have been in 6th-century Ayurvedic medicine in India. Tincture of cannabis was widely prescribed in the Victorian era. In 1915, Dr. William Osler, in one of the seminal textbooks of modern medicine, called it "probably the most satisfactory remedy." British neurologist

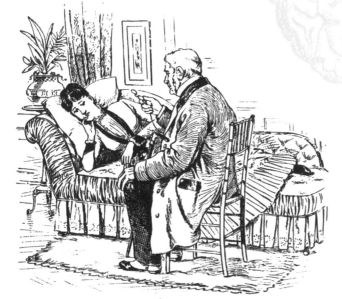

🌿 *A Victorian-era palliative for migraines was tincture of cannabis and "absolute rest."*

Sir William R. Gowers recommended tincture of cannabis and "absolute rest," determining whether it worked and the proper dosage and timing by trial and error. In 1877, the eminent New York neurologist Dr. E.C. Seguin urged preventing migraines by prophylactic use, keeping the nervous system "steadily under a slight influence of cannabis for a long period of time," a course also suggested by Montana neurologist Dr. Ethan Russo, who specializes in cannabis and migraines.

Current migraine research focuses on the neurotransmitter serotonin, with triptan drugs effective at aborting attacks by acting on serotonin receptors. Cannabis and anandamide, the brain's endogenous cannabinoid, have been shown to stimulate some serotonin receptors while inhibiting others, including one that mediates nausea and pain. "Stimulation

Cannabis also has an analgesic effect, and works synergistically with opioid painkillers such as codeine. Like codeine and the triptan drugs, it is most effective if used early—but not too early—in the attack. "Many victims of this malady have kept their suffering in abeyance by taking hemp at the moment of threatening or onset of the attack," wrote Dr. J.R. Reynolds, the physician who prescribed tincture of cannabis to Queen Victoria, in 1890.

As migraines are a complex psychophysiological syndrome that varies from individual to individual, Dr. Gowers' trial and error advice still holds.

🌿 *Pioneering physician Dr. William Osler called cannabis the best remedy for migraines.*

of serotonin 1A receptor subtype helps acute migraine, while antagonism of serotonin 2A receptor subtype helps with migraine prevention," Dr. Russo explains. "Almost no other drug does both. It is also anti-inflammatory and neuroprotective." In 1996, cannabinoids were found to have "antinociceptive" effects, decreasing responses to pain signals, in the periacqueductal gray matter of the brain—an area that suppresses pain, is thought to be involved in migraines, and has a large concentration of endogenous cannabinoid receptors.

## Canada's Mineshaft Pot

In Canada, a series of court decisions from 1997 to 2002, most prominently in the cases of Ontario epileptic Terry Parker and AIDS patient Jim Wakeford, said that the government could not prosecute medical-cannabis users, and ordered it to come up with a legal supply. Ottawa's response was to hire a company to grow marijuana in a Manitoba mineshaft, under tighter security than that required for stocks of Ebola fever virus. The mineshaft pot was a fiasco, far inferior to the herb purveyed at the country's compassion clubs—which are widespread, especially in British Columbia, but still illegal.

# THE STRUGGLE FOR MEDICAL MARIJUANA

In the 1970s, the spread of pot-smoking revived interest in cannabis' medical use. Glaucoma patient Robert Randall found that grass helped relieve pressure in his eyeballs, and successfully sued the federal government for the right to have a legal supply after he was arrested for cultivation in 1975. The result was the establishment of the Compassionate Investigative New Drug program, which still dispenses pot to seven surviving patients.

From 1978 to 1982, 34 states passed medical-pot laws, but the momentum was stilled by the anti-pot backlash of the Reagan era. NORML and Randall challenged the 1970 federal ban on medical use, and in 1988 Francis Young, a Drug Enforcement Administration administrative law judge, ruled that doctors should be allowed to prescribe marijuana, calling it "one of the safest therapeutically active substances known to man." The DEA rejected his ruling.

As AIDS spread in the 1980s, gay men discovered that cannabis' appetite stimulation could help fend off the "wasting syndrome" of the disease. In San Francisco in 1991, Dennis Peron, a longtime pot dealer and gay activist, spearheaded the passage of a medical-marijuana initiative, after his lover died of AIDS. Hundreds of AIDS patients applied to the Compassionate IND program, so President George Bush closed it to new applicants in 1992.

The turning point came in 1996 in California, when Peron and other activists launched Proposition 215, a state ballot initiative allowing use and cultivation by or for patients with a doctor's recommendation. After political professionals funded by billionaire philanthropist George Soros took

*President George Bush at an antidrug event in Delaware in 1989. For Bush I, being "tough on drugs" included closing the federal medical-marijuana program to new patients after it received scores of applications from people with AIDS.*

over the campaign, it won 56 percent of the vote. Arizona voters approved a similar measure the same year, and over the next five years, Washington, Oregon, Alaska, Colorado, Maine, Nevada, and Hawaii also legalized medical pot. (Washington, DC's 1998 initiative got 69 percent of the vote, but was nullified by Congress.)

The Clinton administration reacted harshly to the California vote. It threatened to revoke doctors' prescription licenses if they recommended medical marijuana, a move barred by the Supreme Court in 2003. Some local authorities also refused to recognize the law. Cannabis buyers' clubs, where patients with doctors' recommendations could buy—and sometimes smoke—medical herb, opened across the state. Peron's San Francisco club, one of the loosest at screening patients, was closed in 1998. The city of Oakland tried to authorize its local club as a municipal agency, a move that failed when the Supreme Court in 2001 rejected claims that "medical necessity" could allow people to distribute marijuana legally.

The DEA followed that up with raids on medical growers in California. The victims included the Wo/Men's Alliance for Medical Marijuana in Santa Cruz, the most nonprofit club in the state, and the Los Angeles Cannabis Resource Center, the strictest at screening patients. In 2002, Bryan Epis got 10 years in prison for growing for himself and four other patients in Chico.

However, the federal government has had trouble winning higher profile cases. In 2003, cultivation expert Ed Rosenthal, convicted on charges carrying a five-year mandatory minimum, was sentenced to one day in jail after jurors complained that they had been duped. Defendants in federal marijuana trials are not allowed to mention medical use, because federal law says there's no such thing.

Buyers' clubs persist, especially in Oakland, but there is still no legal source of supply for medical-marijuana users in the United States, except for the seven left in the IND program.

🌿 *Medical-marijuana patients and advocates protest in Washington in 1999. Speaking is Chuck Thomas of the Marijuana Policy Project; on stretcher is multiple-sclerosis patient Cheryl Miller, who died in 2003.*

# CANNABIS SPECIES
# SATIVA, INDICA, AND RUDERALIS

More than 20 different species and subspecies of cannabis have been claimed during the last three centuries, though some botanists insist that there is only one—cannabis sativa. However, the cannabis plant is generally considered to have three species: cannabis sativa, cannabis indica, and cannabis ruderalis.

Cannabis sativa, classified by the Swedish taxonomist Carolus Linnaeus in 1753, is the largest of the three, reaching 5 to 18 feet at maturity. It has loosely spaced branches, and grows best for marijuana in tropical regions—Mexico, Colombia, Jamaica, Africa, and Thailand—though it is also grown for hemp in the temperate zones of Europe and North America.

*Purple Kush is an indica strain descended from plants grown in Afghanistan's Hindu Kush mountains.*

Cannabis indica, classified by French biologist Jean-Baptiste Lamarck in 1783, is much shorter, usually only 3 or 4 feet tall at maturity, and has much denser branches. Native to the Middle East and Central Asia, primarily Afghanistan and Pakistan, it was traditionally grown for hashish.

Cannabis ruderalis, classified by Soviet botanists in 1924, grows in Russia and Eastern Europe. It's tiny—1 to 2 feet tall—and weedy, with few, if any, branches and almost no THC. As its small stature and extremely early maturity would be desirable traits for marijuana, a few breeders have crossed it with other species. However, it is difficult to breed reliably and sustain potency, factors which, as Robert Connell Clarke notes in his introduction to *The Cannabible*, make ruderalis hybrids likely useful only to "outdoor growers at near polar latitudes where little else will grow."

The differences were crucial to the development of marijuana cultivation in the West, especially indoor growing. When North Americans first

tried to plant their Mexican, Jamaican, or Colombian seeds in the 1970s, the results were often disappointing. Tropical sativas' love for intense sunlight and long growing season—five to six months for Mexican, seven or eight months for equatorial Colombian—meant that the first frost (or the police) often arrived before the plants had budded. The growing scenes in the Pacific Northwest and Amsterdam didn't really take off until the acquisition of indica seeds from Afghanistan in the late 1970s.

Indica matures faster and produces smaller plants with bigger buds. They also flower reliably when placed in at least 12 hours of continuous darkness each night, whether from the autumnal equinox or an indoor grower turning off the lights. These are important considerations for growers in the United States, Canada, and Europe, who face a shorter outdoor growing season than the tropics, need to avoid police detection, and want to get the maximum yield out of indoor growrooms.

Today, most marijuana grown in North America and Europe is either indica or an indica–sativa hybrid. Few Westerners have smoked pure sativa in the last 20 years, says *High Times* cultivation reporter Kyle Kushman. Despite the smaller yield from sativa plants, many cannabis connoisseurs prefer them to indicas, as they're generally believed to have a more cerebral, psychedelic high.

🌿 *Fertilizing cannabis seedlings. Most indoor and temperate-zone growers prefer indica plants or indica-dominant hybrids, as they take less time to mature and bud than sativa plants.*

# HEMP

**Hemp is cannabis grown for fiber. It is the same plant as marijuana, but they are radically different cultivars, versions of the plant bred and grown to bring out specific characteristics, and as far apart as a Chihuahua and a Great Dane.**

🌿 *Hemp seeds can be ground to make flour or pressed to yield oil.*

Hemp cultivars usually have minimal THC—some countries limit it to 0.3 percent—while marijuana cultivars are selected for maximum potency. Hemp is also cultivated to bring out diametrically different characteristics from marijuana. Hemp plants are packed densely together, because the stalk is the most valuable part, and males are preferred. Marijuana cultivars must have enough space for buds to spread out, and the females are preferred.

In traditional hemp cultivation, the stalks are "retted" after harvest, left out in dew or rain until they rot. That makes it easier to separate them into the bark, which gives long

🌿 *A backpack and change purse made from hemp, products of the 1990s revival of industrial hemp.*

fibers used for paper, rope, and cloth, and the hurds, the woody core, a source of cellulose. The seeds are used for oil.

Hemp has been cultivated in China for over 5,000 years, and was used to make the first paper. It became a staple crop in France, Russia, and Eastern Europe by the 16th century. "All the wool-bearing trees of India, the cotton vines of Tylos, in the Persian Sea, like the cotton plants of Arabia, and the cotton vines of Malta do not adorn as many people as this one herb," François Rabelais rhapsodized in *Gargantua and Pantagruel*. French peasants said that if you wanted to soften hemp bedsheets, you should give them to newlyweds. A notorious use of hemp was for hangman's ropes, mocked as a "hempen caudle" by William Shakespeare.

Brought to Canada in 1606, hemp became a major colonial crop. Both George Washington and Thomas Jefferson grew it, and it supplied rigging and sails for the Navy and the 19th-century clipper ships. Introduced to Kentucky in 1775, it became the state's leading crop, and it was also grown in Missouri and the Midwestern "corn belt." However, competition from cotton and Asian rope fibers caused cultivation to decline by the early 20th century.

The development of the "decorticator" in the 1930s—a machine that separated hurds and fiber without having to ret the stalks first—might have revived hemp cultivation, but the 1937 Marihuana Tax Act scotched that. After the Japanese took control of much of East Asia and the Philippines during World War II, cutting off the US supply of rope, the Department of Agriculture exhorted farmers to grow hemp again, with a short film entitled *Hemp for Victory*. The Nazis matched that with a booklet telling farmers: "He who grows hemp with industrious hands helps himself and the Fatherland." It's now grown in Canada, China, France, Russia, Hungary, and Romania.

Hemp was resurrected in the 1990s, largely thanks to Jack Herer's book *The Emperor Wears No Clothes*. The hurds are used loose for insulation, or held together with a binder and used for lightweight construction materials. The oil is used in food, lotion, and soap. However, the new hemp-clothing industry fizzled quickly, due to high prices for imported fabric—it's illegal to grow it in the US—and hemp

### Hempen-Necktie Parties

Hemp's strongest historical associations are with the hangman's rope. Pirates in Elizabethan England "danced the hempen jig," while 19th-century Texas outlaws "stretched hemp." Executioners endorsed hemp as the strongest and smoothest rope, and lubricated nooses with wax, oil, or soap.

HEMP PAPER

crusaders' inexperience in the "rag trade." Numerous hemp-based food products were also developed, including pretzels and cheese, but the DEA has banned those containing any trace of THC.

Hemp is also used for rolling papers. For newsprint or book paper, it works better when blended with recycled paper. Widespread use of hemp paper could help save forests. According to a 1916 Department of Agriculture study, one acre of hemp, if the hurds were utilized, could produce as much paper as four acres of trees.

*Capsules of hemp oil: It isn't psychoactive, but contains nutritious essential fatty acids.*

# CULTIVATION

*"I also gave the Gardener a few Seed of East India*
*hemp to raise from, enquire for the seed which has been saved,*
*and make the most of it at the proper Season for sowing."*

George Washington, letter to his farm manager, 1794

**CANNABIS** is cultivated all over the world, from the Netherlands to the Himalayas, from Alaska to Swaziland. While it grows wild in many climates, knowledge, care, and technique are needed to nurture potent smoke, whether it be rubbing off the resins to produce hashish or culling out the males to yield sinsemilla.

Home-growing in the industrialized world has mushroomed with advances in hydroponics and indoor-lighting technology and the development of strains bred for temperate-climate cultivation (plus the market incentive of high prices). Through the 1970s, virtually all cannabis consumed in the West was imported from traditional growing countries like Mexico and Morocco, but now a significant percentage is grown locally, most notably in Canada and the Netherlands.

The amount of cannabis herb (marijuana) and resin (hashish) seized by law enforcement officers in recent years has averaged around 4,000 tons, which means that the total global crop may be 30,000–40,000 tons a year.

# CANNABIS AROUND THE WORLD
# CULTIVATION

**A 1996 Interpol report claimed that 79 countries had cannabis crops big enough to export. Still, the bulk of the global stash comes from a handful of countries.**

Mexico and the United States are the largest producers of marijuana, possibly responsible for more than half the world's weed. Morocco and Pakistan supply most of its hashish, and South Africa and Paraguay are key regional sources of *dagga* and *mota*. Exports from Colombia exploded in the 1970s, but dropped off after the drug trade found cocaine more profitable and easier to smuggle.

## KEY

**TRADITIONAL MARIJUANA-GROWING COUNTRIES**
THE AMERICAS
*Mexico, Jamaica, Colombia, Brazil, Paraguay*
ASIA
*India, Thailand, Cambodia, Vietnam*
AFRICA
*Ghana, Nigeria, Egypt, Democratic Republic of the Congo, South Africa, Lesotho, Swaziland, Malawi*

**TRADITIONAL HASHISH-PRODUCING COUNTRIES**
*Morocco, Egypt, Lebanon, Afghanistan, Pakistan, Nepal, India*

**COUNTRIES WHERE CANNABIS EXPORTATION HAS DECLINED SIGNIFICANTLY**
*Colombia, Lebanon, Vietnam*

**COUNTRIES WHERE CANNABIS CULTIVATION HAS BECOME WIDESPREAD SINCE 1970**
THE AMERICAS
*US, Canada*
EUROPE
*Netherlands, Spain, Switzerland, UK, Germany, Russia*
ELSEWHERE
*Australia*

# CANNABIS AROUND THE WORLD
# CONSUMPTION

As cannabis is illegal in every country in the world, consumption is hard to measure. There are no annual sales reports, and arrest and seizure figures may only indicate harsh laws or transshipment.

A 2002 United Nations report estimated that 147 million people use cannabis at least once a year. The rates were highest in Oceania, where almost one fifth of people 15 and over get high, and lowest in Asia, at 1.6 percent. These figures should be taken with a grain of salt: How many people are willing to tell a quasi-official figure that they use illegal drugs, and how reliable are numbers from war zones, shantytowns, and remote rural villages? Still, surveys, cultural history, and anecdotal evidence give some idea of where pot use is most prevalent.

**UNITED STATES:**
Despite over 700,000 arrests a year, more than 70 million Americans have tried pot, and one out of 12 adults and teenagers use it annually.

**ST. VINCENT AND THE GRENADINES**
May outstrip Jamaica for ganja use.

**JAMAICA:**
Nearly half of men over 15 have smoked herb at least once, but only about one sixth of women have.

## HIGH RATES OF CONSUMPTION

*Papua New Guinea, Micronesia, Ghana, St. Vincent and the Grenadines, South Africa, New Zealand, Australia, Sierra Leone, Zambia, Nigeria, Ireland, UK, El Salvador, Canada, US, Mali, Morocco, Spain, Switzerland, Jamaica, Afghanistan.*

**UNITED KINGDOM**
One research group estimates that sales of British homegrown eclipse those of the country's largest brewer.

**NETHERLANDS**
Closest to legal use of any country, with officially tolerated cannabis coffeeshops, though many cater more to tourists than to locals.

**AFGHANISTAN**
Hashish-smoking is reported near universal among soldiers in this war-ravaged land.

**INDIA**
The UN estimates about 22 million cannabis users, more than any other country.

**ISRAEL**
"We're a tense society, and the Jewish people have never done very well with alcohol," says a leading pot activist.

**PAPUA NEW GUINEA**
According to the UN's 2002 report, 29 percent of adults smoke *spak brus*—the highest amount in the world.

**SOUTH AFRICA**
Heartland of *dagga*.

**NEW ZEALAND**
More than half of people between 15 and 45 say they have used cannabis.

# CANNABIS CULTIVATION AND BREEDING COLONIES

**"In every bag a seed, and in every seed a bag," is an old stoner adage. Homegrow marijuana is cheaper, fresher, and often purer and more potent than black-marke weed, and growers take great pride in having created it.**

Until the late 1970s, virtually all cannabis smoked in the US, Canada, and Western Europe was imported from traditional growing countries. Marijuana was almost all sativa, from Mexico, Jamaica, Colombia, Vietnam, Thailand, and occasionally more exotic locales like the Congo, South Africa, or Brazil, while hashish was Moroccan, Lebanese, Afghani, Pakistani, and Nepalese.

Varieties were identified by location. They came from "landraces," regional cultivars that were inbred and sufficiently adapted to local conditions to have distinctive characteristics. They may have been descended from northern-latitude

hemp, but they were potent—sometimes almost psychedelic—and thrived in tropical sunshine. Among them were the legendary Acapulco Gold and Michoacan from Mexico, Panama Red (which also encompassed similar reds from the nearby Colombian coast), and Santa Marta Gold from Colombia's highlands. (This nomenclature also inspired joke names, like "Sewer Silver," an urban legend about seeds from pot flushed down the toilet during police raids and miraculously sprouting in the sunless sludge beneath Manhattan.)

The first Western attempts at growing in the 1960s and 1970s came from stoners planting the seeds that slipped

🌿 *These young plants are being grown packed together in the "Sea of Green" method.*

down the album cover during rolling up.
They didn't always fare well. Northern
Mexican sativas could grow in the US,
especially in the South, but Colombian and
Thai strains, used to the perpetual summers
near the equator, weren't adapted. Soma,
an American expatriate now running a seed
company in Amsterdam, started out when
the Colombian seeds he threw out his
window sprouted. "I was growing in the
cold climate of Vermont, outdoors, and this
strain could never finish before it froze," he
told "ganja guru" Ed Rosenthal. "That was
my first insight into breeding."

More sophisticated efforts came from
Vietnam veterans who came home with
seeds from Southeast Asia, and California
and Northwestern growers, who in the late
1970s brought back indica seeds from
Afghanistan. In the Midwest, farmers
planted weed in cornfields, in between the
rows—the two plants do well in similar
soil, and the corn is tall enough to
camouflage the cannabis for most of the
season. The Southern Vietnam-vet grower
was celebrated in Steve Earle's 1988

country hit "Copperhead Road," the tale
of a man who returns from Southeast Asia
to grow ganja in the same east-Tennessee
mountain hollow where his granddaddy
made moonshine.

The pot-growing culture was strongest
in California's Mendocino and Humboldt
counties, the remote redwood country north
of San Francisco where a lot of hippies
had moved to "get back to the land."

*🌿 Plants growing in soil in California's Mendocino County, part of the legendary "Emerald Triangle."*

The California growers were among the first to use the sinsemilla technique, culling out the males to stimulate bud growth, and to breed their own strains, such as crossing Colombian and Mexican, hoping to get the Colombian potency and the Mexican growing season. For example, Haze, a 1970s California strain, is a mix of Colombian, Mexican, Thai, and South Indian sativas. Farther north, in Seattle, the rainiest region of the US, growers began primitive indoor gardens using fluorescent lights, and also sought suitable strains.

The indica seeds brought back from Afghanistan proved much more suited for northern-latitude growing. The shorter plants they produced were also easier to conceal, and their shorter growing season—as little as six weeks of flowering—and bushier buds were ideal for clandestine growing in colder climates. "I got a hold of one of those seeds and started growing pure Afghani," Soma recalled in *The Big Book of Buds*. The Dutch also obtained indica strains, such as Chitral from Pakistan.

Law enforcement and lighting technology set off major changes in cannabis in the early 1980s. Paraquat spraying in Mexico, the burning of the fields in Jamaica, and intense suppression of smuggling caused a decline in the quality of imports. Colombian largely disappeared from the US market, along with Thai sticks and Hawaii's legendarily potent sativas. "The effects of exuberant law enforcement on limiting the quality and variety of imported marijuana have been exceeded

*In the 1980s, US-backed military and police forces burned marijuana fields in Jamaica and elsewhere.*

only by greed on the part of producers and smugglers," Robert Connell Clarke wrote in *The Cannabible*. Mexico, one of the first places to grow sinsemilla, is now synonymous with mediocre commercial pot.

In California, helicopter raids in every harvest season handicapped outdoor growing—a greenhouse, used by some growers to lengthen the season, became an automatic bust. As American enforcement tightened, some growers fled to Amsterdam, where the enterprising Dutch developed new strains. As for the rest, "The government pushed us all indoors," an Indiana grower told *The Botany of Desire*

*Despite suppression, Jamaica continues to be a major cannabis producer, and growing methods there have become more sophisticated.*

author Michael Pollan. Indoor growing was also enabled by the new high-intensity discharge lights—metal-halide and high-pressure sodium bulbs, developed in the 1970s for use in sports arenas and streetlights in high-crime neighborhoods.

The result was that cannabis genetics have been globalized and scrambled, as growers seek strains from all over the world, looking for maximum potency, quick maturity, and high yield. However, most current varieties, according to Connell Clarke, are recombinated descendants of a dozen or so strains developed by California and Northwest growers in the late 1970s —Skunk, Haze, Northern Lights, Big Bud—and passed on to the Dutch in the early 1980s, with the occasional admixture of African, Asian, Jamaican, or ruderalis landrace genetics.

For example, Northern Lights is a Northwestern indica, usually grown as Northern Lights #5, a ⅛ Thai cross. Haze, due to its long growing season, is usually used in hybrids, such as Jack Herer, a sativa–indica blend that is 50% Haze, ⅜ Northern Lights #5, and ⅛ Skunk. Blueberry is mostly indica, Afghani crossed with Thai and Mexican Gold sativas. AK-47, an early-1990s Dutch favorite, is about two thirds sativa, from Colombian, Thai, Mexican, and Afghani, touted as having a sativa high while giving a heavy yield in nine or ten weeks of flowering.

*⚕ This early-1990s garden was discovered and destroyed by the Drug Enforcement Administration.*

Breeding cannabis is a complicated process. Many growers prefer simply to use clones, and don't want to sacrifice a season's sinsemilla. This involves growing selected females for seed, with specific males chosen to fertilize them.

The "F1" hybrid, the first offspring of two different plants, will often display "hybrid vigor," the strength gained from a fresh combination of traits. These are hard to keep stable in the F2 and subsequent generations, as undesirable recessive traits are more likely to come out, and traits that require the interaction of several different genes to be expressed can fade out. Thus, breeders will incestuously "back-cross" plants with their ancestors in order to produce a "true-breeding" strain, one with

relatively consistent characteristics. In essence, Connell Clarke writes, modern breeders have "accelerated the age-old natural process by which landraces are created." The ideal is a strain inbred enough to be consistent, but not so inbred that it amplifies defects.

Amsterdam is the most wide-open mecca of cannabis breeding, with seed companies active since the early 1980s and continuous crossing and back-crossing to supply the coffeeshops and global growers. But with indoor cultivation for seeds banned by the Dutch government in 2000, many Dutch breeders are setting up in Switzerland. Spain is also emerging as a European growing center, with loosening laws, hot sun, and cultural ties to Latin American seed sources.

British Columbia, Canada's westernmost province is the world's second main breeding area. It was a logical place for cannabis cultivation to develop, close to the northwestern US sinsemilla belt, with a hippie/pot scene dating back to the 1960s (some say Vietnam war draft-dodgers were among the first B.C. growers); isolated, rainy land for outdoor growing; and cheap hydroelectric power for indoor lights. The province has three main growing areas: metropolitan Vancouver, Vancouver Island off the coast, and the Kootenay Mountains to the east. Quebec is also developing as a breeding center.

With relatively low penalties and much less fanatical law enforcement than the United States, plus the seed-company efforts of militant entrepreneur Marc Emery, B.C. emerged as a major exporter in the 1990s. Local strains include Romulan, a "head-denting" indica named after a ridged-skulled race of *Star Trek* aliens, and Texada Timewarp, mostly indica. However, *Cannabible* author Jason King complains that much B.C. commercial pot, mass-produced in industrial-style growrooms in the Vancouver suburbs, is overfertilized "chemmy indoor no-love bud."

South Africa and Malawi are also emerging as sources, as their temperate-zone sativas have a short growing season. Australian growing began with local hemp from Hunter Valley in New South Wales, but has added Southeast Asian and the usual global varieties. Jamaica, where many growers once just "put it in the ground and let Jah take care of it," now uses Dutch and North American seeds, Alaskan and indica.

In the US, California is by far the leading pot producer, and some old-school sativas remain, such as Gold Rush, a Humboldt County strain descended from Santa Marta Gold. Other leading growing areas are the southern Appalachians, Hawaii, the Pacific Northwest, and Florida. In 1997, NORML estimated that domestic marijuana was worth $15 billion wholesale, the nation's fourth-ranking cash crop—behind corn, soybeans, and hay, but ahead of wheat, cotton, and tobacco. Even if the pot crop were worth only $3 billion, it would still be in the top 10, ahead of potatoes, apples, and oranges.

With indoor growing, cannabis can be cultivated anywhere in the world, with plants and genetics from everywhere. Growers in Argentina can buy seeds from Spain that are descended from Dutch hybrids of Californian and African plants, the Californian a cross between Mexican and Afghani. Yet commercial and police pressures have changed the character of the plant, producing strains that have more THC but are selected primarily for their ability to bloom and sell quickly, before the door gets kicked in. The legendarily psychedelic sativa strains of the past are now gone or rarely grown.

The final product: One large Dutch Skunk bud.

# GROWING METHODS

Cannabis is a weed, but there are hundreds of methods to grow it—still, it's ultimately simple. "Buy some dirt, put it in a pot, and get a light," advises *High Times* cultivation reporter Kyle Kushman. "Plant the seed and watch it grow. Pay attention and take notes." Hydroponic growing is more complicated.

Cannabis needs five basic things to thrive: light, air, water, nutrients, and a growing medium. "Don't worry about becoming an expert," Kushman advises. "Cultivation is all about balance. More is not always more." In general, people who enjoy gardening with other plants will do best at growing cannabis.

## GERMINATION

Seeds need to be planted ¼ to ½ inch deep in soil. To germinate them before planting, one simple and common method is to put them in wet paper towels or cheesecloth. They sprout in two to seven days, and are planted as soon as the root begins to emerge from the seed.

When the seedling is an inch or two tall, it grows two oval leaves called cotyledons. These are followed by single-bladed leaves, three-bladed leaves, and then the plant sprouts the five- and seven-bladed leaves that are its trademark. Sometimes it will grow leaves with nine or 11 blades.

🌿 *Cannabis seeds, ready to be planted or germinated.*

## CLONES

Planting clones—cuttings—allows the grower to get a guaranteed female plant with known qualities. The healthiest, most potent female is used as a "mother" plant.

To make a cutting, an active shoot 4 to 6 inches long is clipped off using sterile scissors, cutting diagonally across the stem. Rooting hormone gives the cutting a good start before planting.

## PLANTING

Plants can be put in small pots at first, but they need to be transplanted—carefully—before the roots get too big for the pot. For growing outdoors, well-drained soil is needed, not too crusty if dry, not too mucky if wet. Soil that grows corn or alfalfa will be good for marijuana.

Kushman advises growers to plan on having a little extra, so they can take the best. Runts should be culled, and the plants should not be overcrowded—it's better to have four with room to grow than ten that are blocking each other's light.

## INDOOR AND OUTDOOR DIFFERENCES

Growing outdoors needs much less technology: If the plants have adequate water, sunlight, and nutrients, nature takes care of the rest. Plants also grow much bigger outdoors. On the other hand, there is less control—for example, you can't force flowering—and the garden can be eaten by insects or deer, stolen by sleazy stoners looking for free pot, or raided. The more accessible it is, the more vulnerable it is to police and thieves.

Indoor growing requires much more work, but the garden is secure, and several crops can be grown in a year. Sophisticated indoor gardens have two rooms, one for the vegetative stage and one for flowering, with separate lights to allow for the different light-cycles needed by plants in those stages. This enables a "perpetual harvest," and the rooms can be as small as upper and lower chambers in a closet.

One technique for indoor growing is called "Sea of Green." This involves growing a large number of small plants, in order to get the biggest yield out of a minuscule space. Flowering is forced when the plants are 6 to 8 inches tall, so they are only 2 or 3 feet tall when harvested.

## HYDROPONICS VS. SOIL

Hydroponic gardening involves growing without soil. The plants are rooted in a neutral medium such as rockwool or

### SEEDS AND PLANTING

Cannabis can be grown either from seed or from cuttings, which guarantees females and shortens the time until flowering.

❶ *Seeds are often germinated in cheesecloth.*

❷ *The seedling first grows round cotyledons, then its first pair of true leaves.*

❸ *Taking a clone by cutting diagonally.*

❹ *A young plant cutting in soil.*

## G R O W I N G

The two main methods for cultivating cannabis are in soil or hydroponically, in a soilless medium.

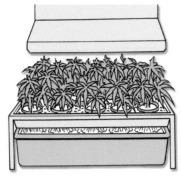

For indoor growers, hydroponics is less messy.

Growing in soil is simpler, but slower.

Cannabis plants need intense light.

coconut fiber, and the roots are bathed in a liquid nutrient solution, whether by dripping or "ebb and flow" periodic flooding and draining.

Growing in soil is easier and more forgiving. Plants cultivated hydroponically grow faster, but gardens can be decimated quickly by a mistake or equipment failure.

## LIGHTS

Cannabis plants growing indoors need light as close to natural sunlight as possible. Regular incandescent lightbulbs won't do, as they generate a lot of heat for the little usable light they produce. Most fluorescent lights are also too weak, although some are adequate for closet-size gardens of three or four plants.

High-intensity discharge lights—metal-halide and high-pressure sodium bulbs—are the best for indoor growing. Metal halides produce more usable light, but some growers prefer high-pressure sodium lights for flowering, as their slightly redder spectrum is closer to autumn sunlight. These lights produce a lot of heat, so they need to be well ventilated, and can burn your eyes if you look directly at them, or explode if touched by water when hot. They use a lot of electricity.

These lights need to be as close to the plants as possible without burning them— plants 4 feet away from the bulb will get less than $\frac{1}{10}$ as much light as plants 1 foot away. Most growers use reflector hoods and either paint the walls of the growroom white or cover them with white plastic. In bigger gardens, lights are put on moving tracks, so all plants get an equal amount of illumination.

A rule of thumb cited by *Indoor Marijuana Horticulture* author Jorge Cervantes is that a garden should produce ½ gram of bud for every watt of light every 30 days—so a 1,000-watt light should be good for a pound a month.

## VEGETATIVE STAGE

This is the stage between the seedling and flowering, when the plant is producing leaves. A healthy plant grows ½ to 2 inches a day. The vegetative stage can last three to five months in outdoor sativas, but is much shorter in indoor indicas.

During the vegetative stage, the plants need the basic nutrients of nitrogen, phosphorus, and potassium (commonly abbreviated as N-P-K), especially nitrogen. They also need lesser amounts of calcium, sulfur, and magnesium, and trace amounts of zinc, iron, manganese, boron, copper, and molybdenum. Plants grow faster with more light, but more than 18 hours a day is overkill.

Fertilizers can be anything from commercial garden products to bat guano and fish meal. Too much will burn the plants. Overfertilizing is a common error among novice growers. Cannabis grown with only organic fertilizers tastes better, but this can be hard to achieve indoors.

## PESTS

Common animal pests include spider mites, aphids, thrips, and whiteflies. These can be avoided by keeping the growroom clean and taking care over what comes in from outside. Cannabis, especially densely budded indica strains, is also vulnerable to botrytis, gray bud mold.

Growers should not use any pesticide that could wind up in the lungs of the people smoking their bud.

## VEGETATIVE STAGE

🌿 The vegetative state is when plants produce leaves and grow taller—it can last for 3 to 5 months.

*Light helps the plants to grow faster during the vegetative stage, but don't overdo it!*

## SEXING

🌿 Determining plants' sex is crucial, as growers who want sinsemilla have to detect and cull the males.

BELOW *Male flowers have a single stamen.*

ABOVE *Females grow pairs of pistils.*

*Manicured homegrown buds, the reward for a season's work.*

### SEXING

When growing from seed, it is essential to cull the male plants in order to get sinsemilla—and the sooner this is done, the less likely it is that they will pollinate the females.

Females tend to be more compact and males more elongated, but most growers say that the best way to tell them apart in time is by preflowers, which appear a week or two before budding begins. Male plants form flowers that look like minuscule bunches of bananas. They first appear as a single green spur tapering to a point, while females grow pairs of white pistils.

### FLOWERING

Most domestically cultivated varieties, especially indicas, require 12 hours a day of *uninterrupted* darkness to flower. Outdoors, this comes from the shorter days after the autumnal equinox. Indoors, it's determined by lighting, and flowering can be forced. Once flowering begins, it takes 6½ to 10 weeks for buds on most varieties to mature.

To avoid a chemical taste in the smoke, growers stop fertilizing and water heavily two weeks before harvest, especially in hydroponic systems. The watering helps to leach out fertilizer.

### WHEN TO HARVEST

Plants need to be harvested at peak potency. Growers determine this by drying a sample bud in the oven and smoking it, or by noting when the pistils at the bottom of the bud are turning brown faster than new ones are growing, or by looking at the capitate stalked resin glands—the trichomes—with a 30x microscope. This is done when the trichomes are fully developed, but still transparent and slightly amber.

Outdoors, harvest is often determined by weather. Heavy rains can damage plants, and dampness encourages bud mold, especially in indicas.

Plants should be cut down rather than pulled out.

# HARVESTING

🌿 When the flowers mature, they must be harvested and manicured, then dried carefully in order to produce high-quality herb.

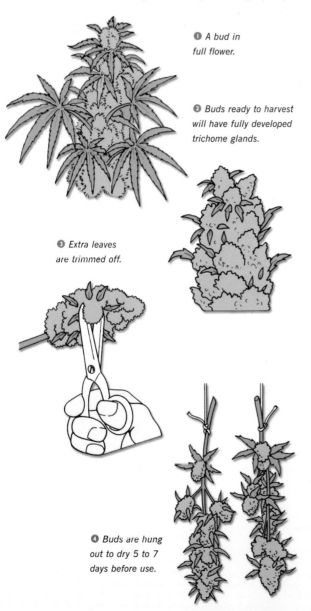

❶ *A bud in full flower.*

❷ *Buds ready to harvest will have fully developed trichome glands.*

❸ *Extra leaves are trimmed off.*

❹ *Buds are hung out to dry 5 to 7 days before use.*

## SECURITY AND "GUERRILLA GROWING"

As cannabis is illegal (and a tempting target for thieves), growers need to be careful that the wrong people don't find out. Ideally, no one should know about a garden.

If growing indoors, the smell is a giveaway, and any suspicious signs need to be hidden from uninvited guests. If growing outdoors, an isolated spot has to be used. In areas where "police in helicopters search for marijuana," growers have to sacrifice sunlight for concealment.

Buying a 600-watt light, an ebb-and-flow table, and 100 cubes of rockwool on a credit card and having it all shipped to the growroom address isn't as blatantly stupid as doing bong hits on the steps of a police station, but it leaves an obvious trail.

## DRYING AND CURING

This is essential for preparing quality smoke. The leaves are trimmed off the buds with small scissors. Care has to be taken not to damage resin glands when handling buds. They are hung upside down in a dark, dry place, warm and ventilated enough to discourage mold. A little warmth will help acid cannabinoids lose a carboxyl group and turn to THC, but too much heat will make the THC degrade to CBN.

When the stems are dry enough to snap—usually after five to seven days—the buds are ready to smoke. They are stored in glass jars, or in plastic bags for freezing.

# SEEDS AND SCAMS

Seed companies play a major role in the cultivation of cannabis, especially of high-end homegrown. Originating in Amsterdam in the 1980s from the network of growers supplying the Dutch coffeeshops, they emerged into the public eye in the early 1990s.

🌿 *A dozen top-quality cannabis seeds can cost more than a quarter-ounce of herb.*

Today, several dozen companies, mainly located in Amsterdam and British Columbia, produce cannabis seeds for sale, among them T.H. Seeds, Flying Dutchmen, Mighty Mite, and Homegrown Fantaseeds. They are distributed by shops, mail order, and scores of Web sites with names like Natural Mystic, Heaven's Stairway, and The Amsterdam Seed Co. (in Vancouver). Canadian pot magnate Marc Emery's seed catalog takes up the first 12 pages of his *Cannabis Culture* magazine, purveying 585 strains from 37 companies. Prices for mail-order 10-packs range from $16 for a generic grab bag to over $300 for top-name strains like NYC Diesel and Jack Herer.

The companies primarily tout their varieties' potency and growing characteristics—indoor or outdoor, length of flowering season, and yield. Most start at about $3–5 per seed, though some strains can cost $10–$15. "Feminized" seeds, which come from female plants pollinated by hermaphrodites and produce almost all-female offspring, command a premium. One Web site that sells Skunk #1 seeds for $46 a 10-pack charges $80 for feminized seeds.

"Delivered discreetly worldwide," the World Wide Seeds Web site says. For White Widow, a Brazilian-Indian sativa–indica hybrid from Amsterdam's Green House coffeeshop, it boasts "intense crystal formation" like "a green plant grown in a snow fall,"

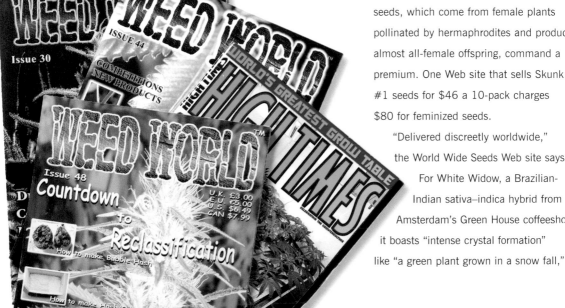

a "serious heavy high," 10 weeks of flowering, and a vegetative stage lasting only two weeks in hydroponic gardens. A 12-pack goes for $105, 94.50 euros, or £66. A 16-pack of Jack Herer, from Amsterdam's Sensi Seed Bank, sells for $154. That strain combines "three of the strongest varieties known to man," but its pedigree remains secret, "just as with the Coca-Cola recipe."

Common problems include seeds getting crushed during delivery, the seeds turning out to be inferior or failing to germinate, or dealers simply keeping the customer's money, whether from dishonesty or spaced-out incompetence. Most seed sellers rely on their reputation; some will make good on defective shipments.

Possession or importation of viable cannabis seeds is illegal in the United States under both state and federal laws. Some companies, such as the Sensi Seed Bank and the British Seed & Read, ship only to Europe.

"We only sell cannabis seeds as souvenirs," is a typical disclaimer, appearing on one British web site a few lines down from its claim to stock "only proven varieties of marijuana seed" and deliver them "promptly and stealthily" to any country in the world. "The lovely F1 cannabis seeds we supply are only to be grown in sensible countries where it is legal to do so, such as Holland, Belgium and Switzerland," says another British site. "If you live in the UK, we will be able to sell you some very expensive fishing bait or budgie food, but you must under no circumstances grow them."

How seeds are concealed is a trade secret. "You have to be able to find your goods well hidden somewhere inside this package," says a Dutch web site.

*In Britain, cannabis seeds are legal—as long as you don't grow them. In the United States, even seeds used in bird food are illegal unless they're sterilized.*

# TECHNIQUES, EFFECTS, AND CUSTOMS

*"These memories do pass critical scrutiny in the morning. I am convinced that there are genuine and valid levels of perception available with cannabis which are… unavailable to us without such drugs."*

Carl Sagan, writing as "Mr. X," 1970.

**THE PRACTICALITIES** of cannabis involve much more than inhaling. There are myriad techniques, tools, and customs. Even something as instinctive for experienced stoners as rolling a joint takes practice.

The mental state of being "lost in the moment," of sensory overtones and serendipitous free association, can be a welcome alternative to concentrating on mundane obligations, but there are consequences—such as being unwilling or unable to deal with those obligations while very high. Perhaps a character in Terry Southern's story "Red-Dirt Marijuana" put it best, when he defined the difference between "workin'-hour gage" and "Sunday gage": "You don't *swing* with you heavy gage, you jest *goof*… you got to be sure ain't nobody goin' to mess with you 'fore you turn *that* gage full on." As rapper Aceyalone said, you have to learn to "master your high."

And as in any other area of life, you'll get on people's nerves if you're selfish or rude.

# USING CANNABIS

Smoking marijuana is as simple as putting on a condom, but learning how to appreciate and manage the high is much more complicated. Meanwhile, ingenious potheads have concocted a multitude of ways to get it into their bodies.

*A 1970s-style plastic bong, a tall, tubular waterpipe of Thai origin.*

## SMOKING

The joint, the hand-rolled marijuana cigarette, is the classic. It's simple to make, requires no paraphernalia other than paper, is easy to pass and dispose of, and is relatively inconspicuous. The most common variations are the spliff, a large, somewhat conical reefer of Jamaican origin, and the blunt, a joint rolled in cigar-leaf tobacco instead of paper.

More exotic creations include multipronged joints and the "tulip," a bulb-sized wrap of ganja toked through a straw or pen barrel. These require large quantities of herb and are hard to get to burn evenly.

The other main method of smoking cannabis is in a pipe. This is more economical, as less smoke escapes, and better for very sticky bud, which is hard to roll in a joint and can burn poorly. Waterpipes, including the bong, cool the smoke and may filter out some toxins, and bongs deliver a mammoth toke.

Hashish is usually smoked in a pipe by Americans. Europeans are more likely to roll a hash-and-tobacco spliff.

One method of smoking hash without a pipe is to heat two knives on the stove and squeeze the hash between them, then inhale the smoke. Another is to stick a small chunk of hash on a pin, light it, and place it under a jar to capture the smoke, and then inhale the smoke.

Trichomes and hash oil are the most potent cannabis products. Trichomes go best in a small pipe, though they can be rolled into a joint. Hash oil can be smeared on a rolling paper or, more efficiently, heated from below in a glass pipe.

## VAPORIZATION

This process involves heating the pot precisely, then inhaling when it reaches the proper temperature. It relies on the principle that THC vaporizes at a lower temperature (356°–392°F or 180°–200°C) than that at which plant matter combusts (446°–455°F, 230°–235°C), and thus spares the user from inhaling the toxins of smoke. This is especially important for heavy medical users. Still, taking a draw without feeling the smoke is disconcerting for many tokers.

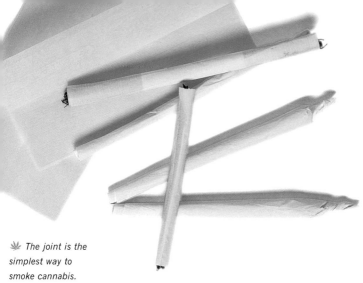

🌿 *The joint is the simplest way to smoke cannabis.*

The technology is still developing. The cheaper commercial models are almost universally despised as a waste. Some people have gotten better results with homemade contraptions involving soldering-iron heating elements and the like. The best current commercial models have digital temperature readouts and cost at least $200.

Aside from cost, the disadvantages are that vaporizers are as bulky as a bong, require electricity, and are conceivably too complicated for use by the extremely baked.

## EATING

Eating cannabis is also healthier than inhaling smoke, and it can make you very high for long periods of time. It's the best way to ingest a large dose, and is especially good for medical users if they can keep it down and don't need instant relief. It's also a good way to use

🌿 *Homebaked goods are a common way of eating cannabis.*

leaves and male plants, which are not very potent for smoking, but still contain THC.

As THC is not water-soluble, the cannabis must be dissolved in alcohol or fat to work. The classic recipes are brownies and other baked goods, but pot can be cooked into almost anything.

It takes at least an hour or two to get off after eating cannabis, maybe even three on a full stomach. Users need to watch out for the "I'm not really feeling it, so I'll eat another" syndrome. Many Amsterdam coffeeshops stopped selling "space cake" after one too many tourists turned into a puddle.

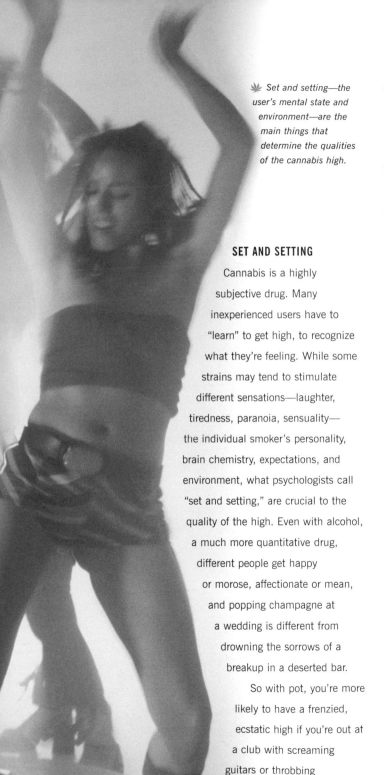

*Set and setting—the user's mental state and environment—are the main things that determine the qualities of the cannabis high.*

## SET AND SETTING

Cannabis is a highly subjective drug. Many inexperienced users have to "learn" to get high, to recognize what they're feeling. While some strains may tend to stimulate different sensations—laughter, tiredness, paranoia, sensuality— the individual smoker's personality, brain chemistry, expectations, and environment, what psychologists call "set and setting," are crucial to the quality of the high. Even with alcohol, a much more quantitative drug, different people get happy or morose, affectionate or mean, and popping champagne at a wedding is different from drowning the sorrows of a breakup in a deserted bar.

So with pot, you're more likely to have a frenzied, ecstatic high if you're out at a club with screaming guitars or throbbing drum-and-bass rhythms, and more likely to have an intellectual high if you're discussing philosophy in a book-lined study. If you burn with your lover in a candlelit boudoir, you're more likely to have an erotic high. If you smoke with people who you fear are cutting you down behind your back, you're more likely to get paranoid. If you lie down with a pipe after getting off a 12-hour shift, you're unlikely to be awake in an hour.

Regular or heavy use can build up tolerance. This is good in that you're not overwhelmed by one or two hits of fine pot, but bad in that it reduces the awe-inspiring nuances of the high down to a mere buzz. If you're getting extremely spaced, it's probably best to do it in a congenial, tolerant atmosphere—unless you thrive on the theatrics of being crazed and incoherent in public.

More is not always more. If you're in Amsterdam, you might be better off smoking one joint at a coffeeshop and then going off to the museum to get mesmerized by Vincent Van Gogh's brushstrokes, rather than smoking nine and being unable to say anything other than "'Ere." Cannabis is supposed to enhance your life, not be your life.

## HEALTH RISKS

No one has ever died from an overdose of cannabis. The long-term effects of cannabis smoke are uncertain. It contains many of the same toxins and carcinogens—benzene and polycyclic aromatic hydrocarbons—as cigarette smoke or other burning plant matter. Some research, most notably that of Dr. Donald Tashkin at the University of California at Los Angeles, has found precancerous abnormalities in pot-smokers' lungs, especially those who also smoke tobacco. However, no case of lung cancer in a cannabis-only smoker had been recorded as of 2002, according to Montana medical-marijuana specialist Dr. Ethan Russo.

Most pot-smokers suffer far less exposure than cigarette smokers, even if they hold the smoke in longer. Very few people smoke 20 joints a day by themselves. A 1997 study by the Kaiser-Permanente health-maintenance organization, of 65,000 patients in the San Francisco Bay Area over 12 years, found that pot-smokers had more respiratory complaints than non-smokers, but did not have a higher death rate.

People who suffer from mental problems such as schizophrenia or depression should be very careful with cannabis, as it can set off feelings of depersonalization or unreality. Pot also makes some people nervous or paranoid—these people usually quit smoking it.

## DRIVING

Cannabis intoxication does not affect driving as much as alcohol. Several studies, most notably one done for the British government in 2000 to test stoned people's performance

on driving simulators, have indicated that pot-smokers are aware that their reaction time is impaired and compensate by driving slower. Still, driving while high is not recommended. You don't want to be merrily tooling down the highway, entranced by the buzz and the rubicund river of taillights, when some arrogant fool in a SUV cuts you off and stops short.

🌿 *Cannabis contains many of the same toxins as cigarette smoke, but few people smoke 20 joints a day.*

🌿 *There is no record that either Fidel Castro, foreground, or 1972 Democratic presidential candidate George McGovern, left, ever smoked weed. You should stay straight while driving, too.*

# CANNABIS AND THE BRAIN

**Although cannabis is the second most widely used recreational drug in the world, how it works in the brain was discovered only recently, and much is still unknown. The THC from smoked marijuana reaches the brain almost instantly.**

*The amount of THC in the brain needed to get high is less than 100 micrograms.*

Absorbed by the lungs, it passes into the blood, and easily crosses the blood–brain barrier. In the brain, it binds to the CB1 cannabinoid receptors. These are primarily located in the frontal cortex, which controls thought; the hippocampus, a center of memory functions; the cerebellum and basal ganglia, which coordinate motion; and the limbic system, which affects emotions. Those locations correspond to the areas of increased blood flow in the brains of stoned people. Only about 20 to 80 micrograms of THC reaching the brain are needed to get high, according to British pharmacologist Leslie Iversen in *The Science of Marijuana*, an amount roughly comparable to the levels of neurotransmitters like noradrenaline.

The CB1 receptor system was discovered in the early 1990s. That inspired a search for the endogenous (naturally occurring) chemical that fits those receptors, as endorphins fit the body's opioid receptors. In 1992, an endogenous cannabinoid called "anandamide" was isolated by William Devane and Raphael Mechoulam, the Israeli scientist who had first identified THC. The brain also produces another cannabinoid called 2-arachidonylglycerol (2-AG). The effects of endogenous cannabinoids are similar to those of THC, and other mammals also have cannabinoids in their brains.

In the nervous system, neurotransmitters flow across the synapse, the microscopic gap between neurons, either stimulating them to send off signals or inhibiting them from firing. The CB1 receptors are presynaptic, located just before the synapse, and anandamide, says neurochemist Dale Deutsch, works "like a feedback mechanism to slow things down," inhibiting the firing of neurons so they don't get overexcited. The brain is known to synthesize endocannabinoids when nerve cells are stimulated by neurotransmitters such as glutamate and norepinephrine; anandamide may also suppress release of some inhibitory neurotransmitters.

## EFFECTS OF THE CANNABINOID SYSTEM

The cannabinoid system's effects are normally subtle, according to Deutsch, former head of the International Cannabinoid Research Society. It is involved in regulating appetite, blood pressure, intestinal peristalsis, pain sensation, and probably vision. It also affects mood—no one knows exactly how yet—and is believed to help the nervous system manage stress and work as a filter for the memory, so it can select what to retain instead of being inundated by a tidal wave of sensory information. Another theory is that it may help people forget traumatic experiences, such as the intensity of the pain of childbirth. Alcohol and opioids also activate the cannabinoid system, part of the reason they give the brain pleasure.

When people consume cannabis, says Deutsch, the THC "overwhelms the system" of CB1 receptors. It stimulates appetite, lowers fluid pressure in the eyeball, and affects the memory filter to cause one of the more notorious effects of cannabis use, short-term memory loss. That is the phenomenon of—uh, what was I going to say?—forgetting what you were thinking a few moments ago. It is probably caused by pot's effect on the frontal cortex, which is thought to be the "executive" of short-term memory, and the hippocampus, which works to convert immediate impressions to longer-term memory. Stoned people generally do worse on tests of memorizing sequences of numbers and words.

Thus, while being high might be perfect for a musician playing a hypnotic, textural two-chord dub-reggae jam, it would be disastrous for one learning a classical piece with numerous time-signature and key changes. However, cannabis apparently does not erase memories already stored.

Different systems metabolize THC and endogenous cannabinoids: THC is absorbed in the liver, while anandamide is broken down by an enzyme called FAAH. One path of cannabinoid-drug research is the search for something to inhibit FAAH—roughly parallel to Prozac's inhibition of serotonin reuptake, but relying on a different mechanism—to increase the body's levels of anandamide. These drugs could be used as non-intoxicating versions of medical marijuana, for stress relief or appetite stimulation. An opposite path is

🌿 *Action of FAAH, the enzyme that breaks down cannabinoids in the brain, in a neuroblastoma cell.*

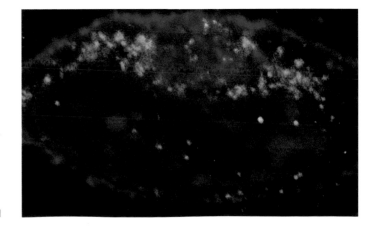

the development of cannabinoid antagonists, chemicals that bind to the CB1 receptors but block them from acting. One called SR140716A could conceivably be developed as an appetite suppressant or memory-enhancing drug, though Deutsch warns that people taking it "might be really irritable." THC and CBD may help reduce brain damage caused by strokes, by protecting neurons from being overexcited by excessive release of glutamate.

The main effects of cannabis intoxication are gone within four hours, and there is no evidence that THC residues remain in the brain. However, a few studies have indicated that long-term heavy users may have subtle problems with cognitive function, primarily in filtering out irrelevant information enough to concentrate on complex tasks. These problems are negligible compared to those caused by similar levels of alcohol use.

*Unlike humans, rats can die from a THC overdose—but it takes a massive amount.*

## IS CANNABIS ADDICTIVE?

Like heroin, cocaine, and amphetamine, THC can activate the release of dopamine—the brain's "pleasure pathway"—but so can food and sex. Repeated or regular use causes tolerance, but the mechanism for that is unknown; it could involve "downregulation" of CB1 receptors in certain parts of the brain. There is also apparently a withdrawal syndrome with cannabis, although much milder than that of opioids. However, as THC takes weeks to disappear from the body, such withdrawal must be set off artificially by administering a cannabinoid antagonist such as SR140716A.

In contrast to opioids, alcohol, and other depressant drugs, there are few receptors for cannabinoids in the brain stem, the region that controls breathing and heartbeat. That is the reason why there has never been a fatal overdose of cannabis in humans. (There is a fatal dose of THC in rats, which have less complicated brains and are more vulnerable, but it comes at levels comparable to a human smoking several pounds of sinsemilla in a few minutes.)

## THE HIGH

The main elements in determining the quality of the high are the set, the setting, and the dose. Low doses are

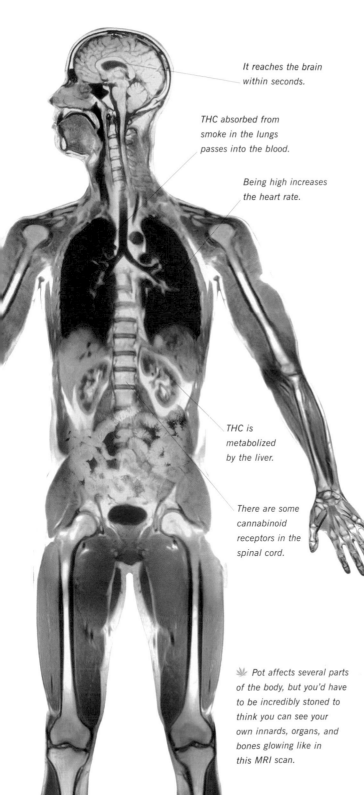

*It reaches the brain within seconds.*

*THC absorbed from smoke in the lungs passes into the blood.*

*Being high increases the heart rate.*

*THC is metabolized by the liver.*

*There are some cannabinoid receptors in the spinal cord.*

🌿 *Pot affects several parts of the body, but you'd have to be incredibly stoned to think you can see your own innards, organs, and bones glowing like in this MRI scan.*

both relaxing and stimulating, and high doses amplify that, tending to be sedative but occasionally provoking paranoia. The passage of time is distorted, usually being perceived as much longer than it actually is. Sensory perceptions are both intensified and dulled, a patchwork effect that can cause the user to wax into a playful, inspired savant or wane into a sluggish, inarticulate slob. Cannabis intoxication also increases deep sleep, but tends to shut off dreams—this is confirmed by both brain-wave measurement and anecdotal accounts.

Iversen calls one aspect of the high "fatuous euphoria"—a concept that is bound to be familiar to anyone who has ever been buttonholed by a pothead prating and preaching about what they are convinced is an epically funny or cosmically profound thought. However, many things that people think, imagine, or feel while high stay valid in the cold light of morning-after sobriety.

Much about the effects of cannabis remains unexplained. For example, no one yet has found the exact reasons why pot can make people laugh, get entranced by music, or feel they have more intense orgasms. Like many aspects of the mind, they lie in the still-mysterious nexus between thought and neurochemical expression.

# PARAPHERNALIA

You can't smoke cannabis without tools. Even the ancient Scythians, inhaling pot smoke in tents centuries before the invention of paper, had bowls to hold the burning buds.

P ot paraphernalia—pipes, rolling papers, and more—has been a multimillion-dollar industry since the 1970s, despite its marginal legal status. Since 1980, the sale of pipes in the US has rested on the legal fiction that the seller has no idea that anyone is using them to smoke pot, and federal law bans "bongs."

Much of the paraphernalia that Westerners take for granted is unavailable in other countries. For example, ganja in Jamaica is sold wrapped in garbage-bag plastic, as zip-lock plastic bags are rare.

## ROLLING PAPERS

The simplest form of cannabis paraphernalia, rolling papers come in myriad varieties. In the 1960s, the bearded smoker on the cover of Zig-Zag papers became an emblem of the marijuana underground. Bambu, another classic brand, became a generic term for papers in inner-city New York in the 1970s and 1980s—"yo, got any Bambu?"—and Rizla occupies a similar position in Britain.

The industry exploded in the 1970s, when you could get papers printed to look like American flags or $100 bills, or in toxic strawberry-pink or banana-yellow flavors. Paraphernalia magnate Burt Rubin marketed a double-sized brand called E-Z Wider, catering to smokers who'd been rolling with two papers stuck together. Intermediate-sized papers—1½ and 1¼— followed. Cheech and Chong did an album called *Big Bambu*, after Bambu's extra-large size. (One wonders if those

*There's a wide range of papers to choose from. Banana-flavored rolling papers (bottom left) were popular in the 1970s. They were taken off the market only recently, when nontoxic flavorings were developed.*

involved knew that "big bamboo" is Jamaican patois for "large penis.")

In Britain, spliff size can be denoted by the number of papers used, as in a "five-sheeter," though four-inch-long spliff papers are available.

In 1972, a California collective called Amorphia sold "Acapulco Gold" papers, made from hemp, to raise money for an unsuccessful marijuana-legalization initiative. The hemp movement of the 1990s naturally revived interest in hemp rolling papers, and today there are several brands available. As a Canadian manufacturer said in 1996, "It's a lot of fun to watch people smoke the stalks with the herb."

*A herb grinder, a useful tool for breaking up sticky buds.*

## PIPES

Pipes are the oldest technique for smoking. Native Americans, who made what may be the first known pipe in western Canada 4,700 years ago, sculpted elaborate stone pipes for tobacco and other leaves. Arabs used hookahs, waterpipes with long hoses, for both hashish and tobacco, from about 1600 on, while ganja-smokers in India used chillums, cone-shaped clay pipes which they later brought to Jamaica.

Pipes specifically sold for cannabis, with a metal screen in the bowl to keep burning cinders from flying into your mouth, emerged along with the headshops of the late 1960s. Small brass or steel pipes, screwed together from plumbing parts, were the staple. They were cheap, but could get uncomfortably hot. Others

🌿 *Three pipes, one of white frosted glass, one a quasi-chillum of wood, and one of gray stone.*

had more exotic shapes, such as skulls and penises. More recently, the British "Raswell" pipe resembles an anodized-aluminum flying saucer. Ceramics, stone, and wood are also used.

Another pipe category is the one-hitter (also called the "bat"), a thin tube with enough room in the end for one or two tokes worth of pot. A common version is made of metal painted to look like a filter cigarette, which helps public smokers avoid detection as long as no one notices it's not burning down. Other "stealth" pipes are shaped like pens, lipstick tubes, or pagers.

When nothing else is available, pipes can be improvised by carving holes into various household objects—soda or beer cans, apples, and cardboard tampon-applicator tubes are favorites—and puncturing pinholes in aluminum foil to make a screen. (The use of tampon-applicator pipes is largely an all-female ritual, due to men's phobia of anything menstrual.)

Borosilicate glass is a popular current material, blown into bats, spoon-shaped hand pipes, and the larger "hammers" and "sherlocks." They feature intricate, multicolored psychedelic swirls. Originating as a hippie cottage industry, with homemade creations sold on the Grateful Dead tour, glass pipes became a big business in the late 1990s. Eugene, Oregon was the glass-blowers' mecca.

## BONGS

Revered by stoners and ridiculed by outsiders, the bong is a waterpipe consisting of a long tube with a small bowl inserted diagonally near the bottom, where the water is. Originally from Thailand, where it was made of bamboo, it arrived in the United States in the early 1970s, and immediately became a hit, due to its ability to deliver a massive toke. Acrylic bongs, sometimes three or four feet tall, stocked the shelves of headshops.

Bongwater, which can smell quite rancid if not changed frequently, is inevitably spilled when some ataxic stoner knocks the bong over. A round-bottomed British bong is called the "Ja Wobbla"— which is also a triple pun on the Rastafarian word for God, the name of reggae-influenced bassist Jah Wobble, and the effects of hitting it too much.

Bongs are the most spectacular examples of the glass-blower's art. The largest and most elaborate, decorated with doughnut-shaped air passages, dragons embedded in marbles, and the like, fetch over $300.

## ROACH CLIPS AND MORE

For potheads who have known scarcity, roaches are too precious to throw away— but they're too small to pass without burning your fingers. Roach clips, devices to hold the roach, are the answer. They evolved out of the bobby pins and electricians' "alligator clips" employed in the 1950s and 1960s. Joint holders and "smoking stones" serve a similar purpose. The "Power Hitter" was a late-1970s product, a plastic squeeze bottle with a joint holder attached to the inside of the screw-on mouthpiece. When you squeezed the bottle, it sent out a powerful blast of smoke.

A useful recent invention is the herb grinder, a cookie-shaped container with spikes on the inside. When the two outside halves are twisted in opposite directions, the spikes break up the herb inside. It's quite practical for rolling fresh sinsemilla, which is usually too sticky to break up with your fingers.

*Roach clips hold the joint when it's too small to pass without burning your fingers.*

*Still life: a glass one-hitter with pot-leaf Mardi Gras beads and a vintage 1970s revolutionary-pothead button.*

# ROLLING
# THE BASIC JOINT

Until pot is legal and you can ask your bartender to twist one up, you've got to roll your own. Prerolled joints have their place in pot history—the "mezzroll" and "panatella" of the 1930s, the cigarette packs sold to American GIs during the Vietnam War, and the "loose joints" of 1970s New York—but they're generally rare. Rolling proper reefers is relatively simple, but it takes some skill. Some people can do it one-handed in a phonebooth in the wind; some never learn. Like anything else, it gets easier with practice. And there's always the alternative of a pipe or a rolling machine.

## PREPARING THE HERB

🌿 For joints to smoke smoothly, the buds must be broken up properly. It doesn't have to be powder, but the pieces should be smaller than a matchhead. If the smoking mix is too clumpy, the joint will go out, be impossible to toke, or "canoe"—burn unevenly, down one side but not the other. (A bit of moisture applied to the faster-burning side may correct this.) Ironically, the best herb is often too sticky to break up easily. A small grinder is a useful tool.

❶ *The seeds and stems will have to be removed. Seeds will either explode or not burn, stems are harsh and can perforate the paper, and neither gets you high.*

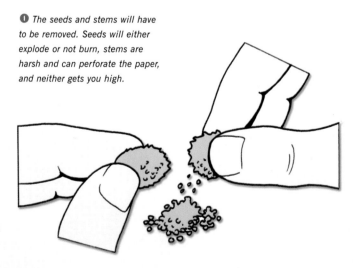

## PAPERS

🌿 Rolling papers come in numerous sizes—single, $1\frac{1}{4}$, $1\frac{1}{2}$, double, and extra-large. The size you use—some people stick two papers together—depends on how big a joint you're creating and your rolling skill. It's easier to roll with more paper, but nobody wants to smoke the phonebook.

❷ *You can use one paper or two (for two, stoners lick the glue on the lower one and put the unglued one on top).*

❸ *The paper should be creased lengthwise, about $\frac{1}{4}$–$\frac{1}{2}$ of the way away from the unglued edge.*

## ROLLING

🌿 The most important part. If the roll is too loose, the joint will fall apart (a minor fire hazard) or canoe, but if it's too tight it won't draw.

❹ *With the glue strip farthest away, a V is formed with the crease and the herb is poured into the V.*

❺ *The paper is rolled up and down between the thumb and forefinger until the herb is distributed evenly. (It's best to do this over something that can catch spilled weed.)*

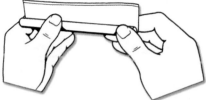

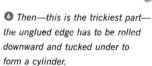

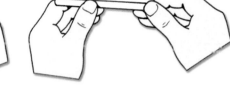

❻ *Then—this is the trickiest part—the unglued edge has to be rolled downward and tucked under to form a cylinder.*

❼ *The glued edge is licked, then the joint is rolled up with gentle pressure (not too loose or too tight) so the glued edge sticks.*

❽ *If the joint is being saved for later, the ends are twisted. Otherwise, a slight space is left open at the mouth end.*

# HOW TO ROLL A BLUNT

To get lifted hip-hop style, the blunt—a joint rolled in a cigar leaf—is a favorite. Named after the Phillies and White Owl "blunt" brands of cigars, they may have originated with the Rastafarian occasional custom of mixing herb and tobacco. They took root in Brooklyn's Bedford-Stuyvesant neighborhood in the early 1980s. By the early 1990s, rappers were celebrating them with tracks like Redman's "How to Roll a Blunt," and Phillies Blunt logo T-shirts were ubiquitous. Preparing the herb for a blunt is similar to what you would do for a joint, except that more is needed.

## SELECTING A LEAF

Phillies and White Owl cigars are the classics. They each have their fans. "Phillies are cool but they burn much quicker," rapped Guru of Brooklyn's GangStarr in 1992. Others use "fronta leaves," cigar wrapper leaves sold separately, sometimes flavored with honey, fruit, cognac, or amaretto. Still others use moist fresh tobacco leaves. These can be quite tasty and may be the most easily tolerated by people who don't like tobacco.

## BREAKING UP THE CIGAR

**❶** *After the cigar has been moistened, it has to be split open very carefully down the middle with a razor blade or the fingers, ideally along where the lines meet.*

**❷** *The tobacco is taken out gently, leaving only the wrapper leaf. The outer part of the wrapper leaf can also be peeled off and the inner one used to roll.*

**❸** *There should be enough herb in it so that there's about half an inch of leaf left for sealing.*

## ROLLING

This is similar to a joint, except that care must be taken not to break the leaf, especially if a cigar is used because it can be brittle.

**❻** *It can be moistened again on the outside to seal it if needed, and then briefly and evenly dried with a lighter.*

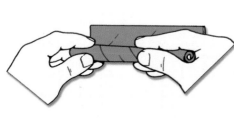

**❹** *It's best to fold the leaf around the trees and then roll, rather than the up-and-down rolling of a regular joint.*

**❺** *Licking the edges and pressing them together should hold the cigar leaves together long enough to smoke. "You have to really make love to it with your tongue," one Web site advises, but Redman's line is "don't drown it with your spit." Honey or liqueur can also help.*

# BUILDING A SPLIFF
# OR EUROPEAN JOINT

While "spliff" is often used as a generic term for a reefer, its specific meaning is a larger, slightly conical joint. Originally Jamaican, it's now spread worldwide. In Britain and continental Europe, the classic hashish-and-tobacco "European joint" has evolved, both through basic similarity and the influence of reggae culture, to resemble the Jamaican spliff. Europeans commonly roll joints with a small cardboard tube inserted at one end, to make it easier to hold.

## PREPARING THE HERB

🌿 Like a joint, only it's bigger, so it's more forgiving of larger pieces of bud. Hashish has to be crumbled into very small pieces. As hash is harder to burn than marijuana, it needs to be much finer than a regular pot joint. Powdery hashes are easy to crumble; the denser black hashes like Afghani and Nepalese are more difficult. They need to be broken into pinhead-sized pieces. It helps to heat the hash briefly with a match or lighter.

❶ *It's important that the cannabis and tobacco are evenly distributed so that people get at least some hash or pot smoke in their toke.*

## ROLLING

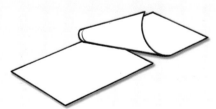

**2** With regular-size papers such as Zig-Zag or Rizla, two can be attached together by licking the gum of one and sticking it on the base of the other. Then a third paper is attached perpendicular to the side of these two.

**3** With extra-long rolling papers, there's no need to do this—you just need one or two. Another method is to put two papers together at an angle of 135° on the gum side, but this can be tricky to roll.

**4** A small holder (known in Britain as a roach) is made by rolling up a strip of thin cardboard (the cover of a book of papers works well), about a ½ inch wide.

**5** The smoking mix is added, with more at the end away from the roach. Some people find it easier to roll with the roach already in; others prefer to insert it after it's rolled.

**6** The main difficulty in rolling it up is getting the conical shape right. Rolling it at a slightly diagonal angle to follow the shape of the pot, not straight up, can help. (One British company sells premade paper cones; all you have to do is drop the herb in.)

**7** A little extra space is left at the fat end. After rolling, the herb is gently tamped down with a pen.

**8** The extra paper is twisted into a "fuse." This makes it easier to light and keeps the weed inside.

# CANNABIS ETIQUETTE AND CUSTOMS

Marijuana manners are more a matter of morality than of ritual. Yes, there are people who say you should always pass it to the left and the like, but such proper-dessert-fork strictures tend to dissipate the more stoned people get. So, pot politeness boils down to three basic rules: Don't be rude; share and share alike—don't be a mooch; and don't do or say anything that will get anyone arrested.

*Etiquette*

1. Don't be rude.
2. Share and share alike; don't be a mooch.
3. Don't do or say anything that will get anyone arrested.

### SMOKING

Passing: Passing customs vary from place to place, and from social circle to social circle. In the United States, people at parties or other private social situations are generally expected to share joints or pipes with others in close proximity. In fact, if you're at someone's house with four or five other people and you don't offer to pass it around, it's considered quite selfish and rude. This is less true in Britain or Jamaica.

If you are at the point where two groups of people intersect and someone passes you a joint or pipe, ask their permission before passing it to the second group. Make sure it gets back to the

🌿 *The etiquette of passing joints varies among different cultures.*

person who lit it reasonably soon, unless they've indicated they don't care.

As cannabis is illegal and often hard to get, it is not as inherently rude to ask someone for a hit off their joint as it would be to ask a stranger in a bar for a sip of their beer. How permissible this is varies greatly, depending on the situation. It's most likely to be acceptable at a private party, or at a hippified cultural event like a pot rally, festival, or jam-band concert. It's least likely to be acceptable in public, or if there's any aura of parasitism or intimidation attached to your request. Social skills and intuition are the key; someone standing two feet away from you is more likely to offer a toke than someone off in an out-of-the-way corner.

If someone turns you on to their pot, don't forget them when you light up some of your own later. If someone gets you high

Waterpipes are traditional in the Middle East for both tobacco and hashish.

regularly, try to smoke them out at least once in a while, even if they're a grower and you make minimum wage. If you ask someone for a light or rolling papers, it's polite to offer them a hit.

Americans generally take one or two hits before passing. Europeans often prefer three or four, and Moroccan kif-smokers usually finish a sebsi bowl themselves. The "take two and pass" maxim is flexible, particularly for a newcomer who isn't as high as everyone else, but don't be a hog, especially if it's not your pot.

Don't ramble on in a lengthy monologue while the joint slowly burns away and other people are waiting for a toke. Pass it!

Don't slobber on the joint or pipe. And if you're lighting a pipe, try to leave a little of the green on top for the next person, rather than scorching the whole bowl.

Traditional hippie style involves sitting in a circle and passing it around, but this varies according to the geography of the space.

Spiritual or religious users often touch their heart and then their forehead after hitting the pipe, in praise and reverence for Jah blessing with the herb. The touch to the heart is for love energy, and the touch to the forehead implies a mental prayer of thanks for the herb.

In general, it's better to err on the side of generosity than on the side of stinginess. Above all, don't spill the bongwater!

## JOINT SIZE

There are regional stereotypes about how thick people roll their joints. Californians, who live in the top pot-producing state in the Union, like to roll redwood-sized doobies. Texans, whose state is awash in cheap but not particularly potent Mexican, also roll fat ones. "It's $55 an ounce, but I've got to roll a hog leg to get high," says one Lone Star State stoner. And in New York City, where pot is almost as pricey as rent, reefers are often anorexic—hence the saying, "You can pick your teeth with a New York joint."

## TOBACCO

Except for blunt-smokers, Americans almost never mix tobacco and herb. Jamaicans mix the two occasionally; some Rastafarians believe that tobacco and herb complement each other yin-yang style. Moroccans mix kif and tobacco.

In Britain and continental Europe, marijuana was rare until the rise of Dutch growing in the 1980s. Hashish, smuggled overland from Nepal, Pakistan, and Afghanistan or across the Strait of Gibraltar from Morocco, was much more common. So the usual method of smoking was a large hash-and-tobacco mix known as a "European joint." Bill Clinton was not the only American to toke on a European joint and cough his guts out. (According to some rumors, the future President Didn't-Inhale then developed a taste for hash brownies.)

🌿 *Bill Clinton couldn't handle inhaling British hash-and-tobacco joints. No one ever asked him if he ate cannabis…*

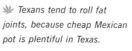

🌿 *Texans tend to roll fat joints, because cheap Mexican pot is plentiful in Texas.*

Even though pot is now widely available in Europe, many people still smoke it with tobacco. Some do it because the tobacco makes the spliff burn more smoothly, or because they like the nicotine buzz added to the pot high. Others prefer the tobacco mix, even though it's difficult to inhale deeply, because it keeps their high at a sociable level, instead of being couch-locked obliteration.

## BUYING

Don't say anything indiscreet on the phone, whether it's "got any smoke?" or ill-conceived code like "how much for a quarter, uh… pound of, uh… cherries?" Don't reveal your dealer's identity to anyone who doesn't know it, or introduce new customers to them without their permission. If someone cops for you, or hooks you up with their dealer—especially if they're not making a profit on the deal—either get them high or give them a nug or two out of the sack.

## HEADSHOP

In the United States, stores that sell pipes and rolling papers operate under the legal fiction that no one uses their wares to smoke marijuana. Yes, it may be a three-foot glass bong covered in psychedelic swirls, sitting in front of a poster of Bob Marley with a giant spliff, but the sign on the wall still says, "All Smoking Accessories Are Intended for TOBACCO Use Only."

Therefore, the number-one rule is: Do not do anything to disturb this legal fiction. If you ask for a "waterpipe," you're OK. If you ask for a "bong" or a "hash pipe" and the store lets you buy one, the law calls it "sale of drug paraphernalia." It's better to point and say, "Can I see that little one" than to ask, "How about that one-hitter?" Also, if you put it in your mouth, you bought it.

## GROWSHOP

Similar rules apply here. If you ask a garden-supply shop clerk, "What kind of hydroponic system works best for pot?" or "Which is better for the bud stage, metal-halide or high-pressure sodium lights?" you're asking them to join you in what the Feds call "conspiracy to manufacture a controlled substance."

Do your research on your own, be discreet, and pay cash.

*⚘ When buying gardening supplies, talking about cannabis could get you thrown out of the shop.*

# THE CANNABIS CONNOISSEUR

*"Aqui, Jeronimo. ¡Fume esta! ¡Te pone muy loco!"*
*("Here, Jerry. Smoke this! It'll make you very crazy!")*

Mexican marijuana farmer to writer-smuggler Jerry Kamstra, 1968

**CANNABIS** has come a long way from the days when people would buy whatever was available, whether it was decent-quality Mexican, spectacular Vietnamese, or sugar-soaked garbage. Today, there are several festivals devoted to cannabis connoisseurship, from the Amsterdam Cannabis Cup and the Vancouver Tokers Bowl, each sponsored by rival marijuana magazines, to local—and often clandestine—events in the Netherlands, Quebec, and California.

Growers breed for taste, smell, and appearance as well as potency and rapid yield. There are scores of named strains, and pot obsessives debate their qualities with the fervor of oenophiles.

Still, many, if not most, North American pot-smokers rarely see the name strains or taste the fruits of the Humboldt County harvest. They are far more likely to encounter commercial-grade Mexican marijuana or Canadian sinsemilla, just as the corner store carries six-packs of Budweiser and Molson, not fresh-out-of-the-barrel exotic microbrew. But they can dream. And when they come across something special, they appreciate it.

# SEEDLESS WONDER
# THE SINSEMILLA STORY

Sinsemilla, from the Spanish word for "seedless," is marijuana specially cultivated to grow without seeds. The reason for this is that female cannabis plants produce sticky THC-containing resin to catch the pollen from the male plants.

Once they are fertilized, they turn their energy toward producing seed. But if the male plants are removed, and there is no other source of pollen affecting the garden, the females keep growing bigger buds and secreting more resin, making the resultant pot much more potent.

The technique was developed in India sometime before 1800, according to botanist Robert Connell Clarke, and had reached Mexico by 1960. Mexican sinsemilla was both extremely potent and stimulating, one former smuggler told writer Paul Krassner, but also extremely pricey; in

1961, when pot sold for $8 a kilo in the Mexican interior, he paid $80 for 250 grams of "sinueso," "boneless" pot. By the late 1960s and early 1970s, as North American potheads were becoming more connoisseur conscious, sinsemilla from Michoacan and Oaxaca began showing up occasionally on the US market, along with legends about how it was grown only by women in the high Oaxacan mountains. Thai sticks were also seedless.

Cultivation expert Jorge Cervantes, who smoked his first sinsemilla in Mexico in 1975—"Popo Blue," supposedly grown on

The mountains of Oaxaca in Mexico, one of the first places where sinsemilla cultivation became common.

the slopes of the Popocatepetl volcano—
called it "the revelation" and "a godsend."
The only problem, he added, was that "the
Mexicans figured there was only enough
sinsemilla for them, and it seldom made
it outside of the country."

That changed quickly. California and
Northwest growers picked up the sinsemilla
technique in the early to mid-1970s, and it
soon became entrenched throughout the
weed world. In Humboldt County, growers
were "culling out males with the fervor of
futuristic lesbians," as Steve Chapple put it
in *Outlaws in Babylon*. Introduced to the
Netherlands around 1979, sinsemilla
caught on there just as local pot cultivation
was beginning to boom. In 1980, Tom and
Nancy Alexander, an Oregon couple who
had opened a garden-supply store after
getting busted for growing, began
*Sinsemilla Tips* magazine, which would
become known as "the trade journal of the
domestic marijuana industry." Jamaican
reggae artists sang paeans to the seedless

like Barrington Levy's "Under Mi Sensi,"
and in 1987, British MC Pato Banton
drew the line against the emblematic drug
of the decade when he sing-songed, "I do
not sniff the coke, I only smoke sinsemilla."
Street dealers in New York hissed "sinse,
sinse," at passers-by.

Today, except for pot cultivated
specifically for seed, the vast majority
of marijuana grown in the Western world,
and virtually all indoor bud, is sinsemilla.
Gardeners growing from clones use all
female plants—they often speak of "the
ladies" or "my girls"—to produce it.
(They do have to watch out for plants
that turn hermaphroditic.)

This is a matter of economic logic.
Pot buyers don't want to pay $350 for an
ounce that can be up to half seeds by
weight, or spend time cleaning out seeds.
And if growers are going to do the work and
take the risks of illicit cultivation, they want
to be rewarded with the best price, the
biggest buds, and the most potent smoke.

# THE SWEET SMELL OF SKUNK

Skunk is one of the legendary strains of marijuana developed in California in the late 1970s, renowned to the point where it has become a generic term for top-quality pot in Britain. It is marked by its dank, strong odor, like a very mild version of the powerfully foul stench that skunks spray to ward off predators.

A stoner joke is that the way to tell a hardcore pothead is if their reaction when they pass through a particularly redolent stretch of road is to exclaim, "Hey, man, smells like good bud!"

The strain known as Skunk #1 is a classic sativa–indica hybrid, 75% sativa and 25% indica, stabilized around 1978. It was originally a cross between 25% Afghani, 25% Mexican Acapulco Gold, and 50% Colombian Gold; sometimes Thai is also bred into the mix. Terpenoids found in the Afghani give it the skunky odor, although current Dutch versions often lack that aroma. "Blooms with long, thick buds, varying in color from light green to golden. Very high flower to leaf ratio," the Dutch Passion seed catalog boasts. "This variety serves as a standard against which others can be measured."

Skunk #1 was created during the era when California and Northwestern growers were crossing Latin American and Asian sativa varieties with Afghani indica strains to produce plants that would grow well indoors and in northern climates—the time when "the modern American marijuana plant was born," writes Michael Pollan in *The Botany of Desire*. "Even today the sativa x indica hybrids developed during this period—including Northern Lights, Skunk #1, Big Bud, and California

*Some pot might smell "skunky," but not this pungent!*

🌿 *Dutch Skunk buds. Amsterdam breeders sustained the genetics after the original seeds were brought over from California.*

Skunk #1 has had scores of successors, among them Skunk 18.5, Super Skunk (a Dutch Skunk/Afghani hybrid), Island Sweet Skunk, Red Skunk, Special Skunk, and Ultra Skunk, a Canadian Big Bud/Skunk cross. It has been crossed and recrossed with Northern Lights, Haze, Afghani, Hawaiian, and other varieties, finding its way into such strains as Bubblegum, Silver Haze, Ice, and Jack Herer. Shiva Skunk is an indica-heavy Skunk/Northern Lights #5 mixture, while Master Kush is a Skunk/Afghani hybrid first grown in an Amsterdam highrise around 1990. Jason King in *The Cannabible* calls Skunk #1 "the backbone of the modern cannabis breeding world."

Orange—are regarded as the benchmarks of modern marijuana breeding; they remain the principal genetic lines."

However, it might not have survived, might have been hacked down and exterminated in the California drug raids of the 1980s, if it hadn't been brought to Amsterdam—by, according to legend, a strange American grower nicknamed "The Skunk Man." Eddy, the Flying Dutchmen seed company's breeder, grew it in a greenhouse in 1984, and "the results were so astonishing, Eddy knew he'd found the future of Dutch weed," Ed Rosenthal writes in *The Big Book of Buds*. "The combination of Afghani and sativa genetics brought together the best of both worlds." Specifically, the Skunk #1 had the clear, cerebral high of a sativa and the heavy yield and rapid flowering of an indica.

🌿 *Skunk #1, the "backbone of cannabis breeding."*

# TRICHOMES

Trichomes, the glands that produce more THC-containing resin than any other part of the plant, appear to the naked eye like white crystals on the outside of the bud, like a dusting of sugar. They are noticeably smaller than the red-hair pistils that are often taken as a sign of potent sinsemilla.

Trichomes come in three types: bulbous glandular trichomes, capitate-sessile glandular trichomes, and the largest, capitate-stalked glandular trichomes. Of these, the capitate-stalked trichomes are the ones that are most responsible for producing resin.

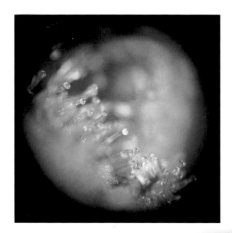

*Lost in the green jungle: A photo-micrographic closeup of trichomes turns into a fish-eyed fantasia, a lush, microcosmic rainforest.*

Capitate means "headed," and their structure—partially apparent at 26x magnification, and fully visible at 60x—is a transparent sphere on top of an equally clear stalk. As the plant matures, they gradually turn darker, amber, and then brown.

Trichomes can be collected by crumbling buds onto an extremely fine sieve over a piece of glass. The pinhead-sized particles make an extremely potent smoke. Even jaded growers, the kind who'd scoff "schwag" at weed that would propel the average stoner out beyond the seven rings of Saturn, consider trichomes a treat. With the possible exception of extremely well-refined hash oil, they're as close as it gets to smoking pure THC.

*Psychedelic dew: This 60x shot shows a microscopic horizon of clear-stalked trichomes.*

🌿 *Dried trichomes removed from the bud and collected on a mirror, ready to be put in a pipe and smoked.*

🌿 *Field of dreams: Trichomes adorn the small tendrils of a green bud almost ready for harvest.*

# CANNABIS APPRECIATION

There are two kinds of pot-smokers, says cultivation expert Kyle Kushman. The first are the average potheads, who just want to get high and hope their weed tastes good. The second is what he terms "cannabiphiles," who can spend hours discussing the nuances of taste and high. The difference is akin to the one between ordinary music fans who like a fat bass sound and audiophiles who can hear a 3-decibel boost in the 62 Hz band.

Smell and taste are the primary aesthetic elements. Canadian breeder DJ Short, in Ed Rosenthal's *The Big Book of Buds,* identifies four basic groups of marijuana flavors: sweet, which encompasses floral and fruity scents; spicy, with piney or sagelike aromas; musky, from earthy to skunky; and chemical/astringent, which includes turpentine and ammoniac odors (there is one strain called "Cat Piss").

The method of smoking also affects taste. In *The Cannabible,* author Jason King notes that some strains taste better in a joint, while others are better appreciated in a pipe or bong, and the flavor of some comes out only in a vaporizer. Stickier marijuana burns more easily in a pipe.

Most important is the quality of the high. "You never hear wine connoisseurs debating the buzz," notes Kushman. The true cannabiphile, he says, can tell the differences between cannabis indica and cannabis sativa, among different kinds of sativas, and distinguish "morning," "evening," or "late-night" grass.

In an ideal world, people could choose among strains of pot based on the kind of high they delivered: laughing, creative, sensual, cerebral, aphrodisiac, sociable, spiritual, or hallucinogenic, some to relax and some for medical use. These elements definitely exist, but they are unpredictable and difficult to define objectively. Even before the subjective nature of the cannabis high is considered, there are a dizzying

*An Amsterdam coffeeshop's selection of "Nederweed" and hashish.*

number of variables involved when whatever intrinsic qualities the pot has meet the smoker's personality, mood, and brain chemistry, their set, setting, and spirit. And in a cannabis-festival atmosphere, where someone might take hits off eight joints and five pipes of different strains in a few hours, the nuances of the buzz from each will be far too jumbled to judge.

Proper storage and handling is another element of cannabis appreciation. Rough handling will knock trichomes off the bud. THC degrades when exposed to heat, moisture, and light, and the chemicals that determine flavor and aroma also dissipate. *The Cannabible* suggests three

different kinds of storage, depending on how long the herb is to last. For small amounts that are likely to be smoked soon, "a dark, dry place is sufficient." For a stash that will last up to a month, refrigeration is the best method of storage, "preferably in sealed glass jars." For longer-term storage, the freezer will preserve buds reasonably well. However, the book recommends not taking the stash out of the freezer too often, because it will draw moisture to the outside of the buds.

> ### *A Question of Taste*
>
> Many people prefer the taste of soil-grown buds, as hydroponic herb that has not had the fertilizer properly "flushed" before harvest often has a chemical flavor and burns poorly.

🌿 *Plastic pot-leaf necklaces: Realistic enough to get your car stopped if you leave them on the dashboard.*

# CANNABIS STRAINS

**Cannabis users, at least the more affluent and better-connected, can choose among hundreds of strains. Most are bred and cultivated primarily for yield and potency, with occasional compromises like accepting four more weeks of flowering to get the high of a sativa-dominant strain.**

*🌿 Cannabis strains are not as well defined as wine varietals.*

S till, the general concept of strains is tantalizing. People wish they could pick a California Haze, a B.C. Romulan, or a Jamaican lambsbread, each with a distinctive flavor and high.

Is marijuana like wine, where drinkers can pick scores of distinct varietals and regional versions of them, from a French merlot to a California zinfandel, a German riesling or a Chilean chardonnay? Or is it more like tomatoes, in which a juicy, organic fruit fresh off the vine will taste infinitely better than a gas-ripened agribusiness product bred mainly to withstand long-distance trucking, but where specific strains are of interest only to gardeners? The truth is somewhere in between. There are definite differences of taste among marijuana

strains, and variations in the quality of the high—especially relative to sativa and indica content—but these are not always consistent. While oenophiles can say a wine has "a fruity bouquet and full-bodied flavor, and goes well with pasta," it's difficult to predict the equivalent for pot—"a fruity aroma, slightly harsh smoke, and a long-lasting high good for music"—as much as people wish they could.

One reason is that pot strains are not as definitively fixed as wine varietals. Despite the suggestions of French cannabis activists, marijuana strain names are not regulated under the "appellation controlée" system, like Beaujolais or Champagne. Another is that the nature of the high is very subjective. A third reason, says Kyle Kushman, is that although genetics are important, even with two plants from the same seeds, "the grower's going to affect what you're smoking more than anything."

Much depends on their skill in creating a favorable artificial climate and harvesting the herb properly. It may be superstition to say that love helps plants grow better—or, as one well-known breeder told Chris Simunek in *Paradise Burning*, that a grower's greed impaired the high from their pot—but care and attention certainly create better bud than industrial-style cultivation. How the constituents of herb affect the high is unknown; a higher THC percentage does not necessarily mean better weed.

Most of the strains commonly available, the ones sold by Dutch and B.C. seed companies, are mainly descended from 10 to 12 original sources. This has caused some observers to complain about homogenization. Kushman counters that the number of possible crosses from those originals expands exponentially with each new generation, and every offspring is unique. *The Cannabible*'s estimate that there are 250 viable and distinct current strains may be true for verifiably stable strains from reputable suppliers, he adds, but there are thousands of growers who know what they're doing and aren't out in public.

Much of the mystique of strains comes from those growers, who constitute a large part of the cannabis subculture and comprise many of the plant's most obsessive devotees. They have created their own potent, tasty,

and euphoric strains, such as South Central Twist from Los Angeles, 911 from Michigan, and Gold Rush from Humboldt County.

The following pages show 20 top cannabis strains, comprising classics and newer favorites from the US, Amsterdam, Canada, and Afghanistan. As there are plenty of great strains from South Africa, Jamaica, and elsewhere, this is by no means an exclusive list.

🌿 *A Dutch indoor growroom.*

🌿 *Black, brown, and beige: several varieties of hashish.*

# SUPER SILVER HAZE

*The Cannabible* calls this sativa–indica hybrid "the Dom Perignon of cannabis," while *The Big Book of Buds* calls it "a stash for all seasons." Created by the legendary Dutch breeder Nevil, it contains Skunk, Haze, and Northern Lights. Pungent and potent, it grows best hydroponically, but can be cultivated outdoors below 35° latitude.

## Drug Testing

As cannabis metabolites can stay in the system for a month or longer, random drug tests are more likely to snare pot-smokers than other drug users. The most common test used is the Enzyme Multiplied Immunoassay Technique urine test, which has a high rate of false positives. There are numerous products intended to foil such tests—one, the Urinator, is a prosthetic penis that emits warmed urine concentrate—and their makers and the testing companies continually vie to outwit each other. For potheads who can't tell their employer to piss off, drinking a lot of water and not giving the first urine of the day can improve the odds.

## CULTIVATION NOTES

 **GENETICS** SATIVA/INDICA

 **GROWN IN** NETHERLANDS

# PURPLE KUSH

Purple Kush is a thick, strong indica with naturally purple leaves and produces a high that is described as heavy and mellow. This strain is grown hydroponically by Trichome Technologies in California.

### Purple Craze

Pot leaves turning purple is normally not a good sign, as it can indicate phosphorus deficiency or weather stress. The exceptions are several strains that are naturally violet, including Purple Haze, Purple Power, and Purple Star. The color purple doesn't make the herb any more potent, but it's beautiful.

## CULTIVATION NOTES

GENETICS   INDICA

GROWN IN   CALIFORNIA

# G-13

This is an extremely potent indica widely—and almost certainly mistakenly—believed to be descended from a clone purloined from the US government pot farm in Mississippi. Grown by Trichome Technologies in California, which says one sample tested at 27 percent THC.

## Snitches Get Itches

Marijuana growers in California's Humboldt County, where the economy runs on logging and sinsemilla, tell the story that when narcotics agents stayed at a local motel during the area's harvest season, the maids rubbed poison oak on the bedsheets in their rooms.

### CULTIVATION NOTES

GENETICS   INDICA

GROWN IN   CALIFORNIA

# STRAWBERRY COUGH

An East Coast favorite—it was quite popular among *High Times* staffers—this is a fruity-tasting, mostly indica plant. It matures quickly, flowering in six to eight weeks indoors, and can be grown outdoors in northern climates. It may be descended from Strawberry Fields and Haze.

## Weed Deliver

In New York and other large cities, those with the right connections can have pot delivered to their door by bicycle couriers, although it usually costs more than it would from a regular dealer. One of the first delivery services—and the most notorious—was founded in a Lower East Side squat around 1981 by Mickey Cesar, a flamboyant, eccentric dealer who called himself "the Pope of Pot." In a combination of self-promotion and civil disobedience, he announced its toll-free phone number— (800) WANT-POT—on the Howard Stern radio show. Cesar, 53, died in 1995, not long after his release from prison.

## CULTIVATION NOTES

**GENETICS**   INDICA DOMINANT
**GROWN IN**   UPSTATE NEW YORK
or MASSACHUSETTS

# SKUNK #1

The classic sativa–indica hybrid, 25% Afghani, 25% Mexican Acapulco Gold, and 50% Colombian Gold. One of the original California strains of the late 1970s, it remains a seed-company staple, both on its own and for breeding. It's generally an indoor plant, but can be grown in a greenhouse; flowering takes seven to 11 weeks.

### New York's Pot Stores

The dream of being able to buy marijuana in stores was a reality in many of New York's poorer neighborhoods in the late 1970s and early 1980s. Storefronts disguised as groceries (their windows blocked by extremely dusty cans of red kidney beans), candy shops, or reggae-record stores retailed reefer in $3, $5, $10, and $20 bags from behind bulletproof partitions. One, a video-game arcade in Brooklyn's Flatbush neighborhood, sold herb through a hole in the wall. The most notorious one was the Paradise Plum, a basement candy shop on East 14th Street in Manhattan. Police closed most down around 1982, but a few survive.

## CULTIVATION NOTES

 **GENETICS**  75% SATIVA

 **GROWN IN**  NEW YORK CITY, 1989

# NORTHERN LIGHTS

The pioneering Northwestern indica, an inbred and not too stable Afghani that can carry a knockout couch-lock high. It matures quickly, flowering in as little as 40 days, and is generally considered easy to grow. One B.C. breeder calls it "perfect for the novice grower," and it has also been used in scores of hybrids. From Trichome Technologies.

### Stoner Darwin Awards 1

In 2002, a Chattanooga, Tennessee man was busted drying his stash in a convenience-store microwave oven—a few feet away from where a police officer was drinking coffee. Police said he told them, "it was a Twinkie." The 34-year-old defendant also had a pound of weed in his car.

## CULTIVATION NOTES

- **GENETICS** INDICA
- **GROWN IN** CALIFORNIA

# SOMA SKUNK

One of several variations on Skunk bred by Soma, an American expatriate grower in Amsterdam. This version has somewhat more indica than basic Skunk.

## Call the Cat Piss Detector

Another marijuana strain whose odor resembles something normally considered foul-smelling is called Cat Piss. An ammoniac aroma usually indicates rotted pot, but this strain reeks like an unchanged litterbox while packing what *The Cannabible* calls a "pulsating and almost overpowering" high.

## CULTIVATION NOTES

**GENETICS** INDICA/SATIVA

**GROWN IN** NETHERLANDS

# KRYPTONITE

A California indica strain. Grown by Trichome Technologies. Not that common, but has become a slang-term generic for incapacitating weed.

## Drug Testing Kids

In 1995 and 2002, the Supreme Court ruled that public high schools could legally require drug tests for students engaged in sports or other extracurricular activities. The Court held that because children were involved, the constitutional protections against searches without probable cause—or even reasonable suspicion of drug use—didn't apply, and that schools did not have to give any evidence that testing "will actually redress the drug problem." Bush administration drug czar John Walters is now advocating extending drug-testing to all secondary-school students, a policy adopted by the town of Lockney, Texas in 2000, but dropped after one family challenged it as an unconstitutional invasion of privacy.

## CULTIVATION NOTES

 **GENETICS** INDICA

 **GROWN IN** CALIFORNIA

# HASH PLANT

A hashy-tasting classic, this version is an Afghani indica with a bit of Northern Lights mixed in. *The Big Book of Buds* says it has "a pleasantly narcotic high." It flowers in about six weeks. Grown from seeds from the Sensi Seed bank in Amsterdam.

### Pipe Gunk

Contrary to stoner folklore, the black gunk that collects in well-used pipes is not "resin." It's mostly tar, and won't get you high if you scrape it out and smoke it. If it did, you could also get off drinking bongwater.

## CULTIVATION NOTES

 **GENETICS**   INDICA/SATIVA

**GROWN IN**   NEW YORK CITY

# AFGHANI HASH

This is "shoe hash," smuggled across the border in the heel of a shoe, thus producing its lumpy, leathery texture. Afghani black hash, much prized in the 1970s, reappeared on the US market after the fall of the Taliban in late 2001.

## We Should be So Lucky

Marijuana use, said Reagan administration drug czar Carleton Turner in 1982, is a behavioral pattern associated with "involvement in anti-military, anti-nuclear power, anti-big business, anti-authority demonstrations." In 1998, schools in Salt Lake City, Utah gave parents a booklet—endorsed by prohibitionist Sen. Orrin Hatch—called "How Parents Can Help Children Live Marijuana Free," which warned that "excessive preoccupation with social causes, race relations, environmental issues, etc." was a sign of teenage drug use. On the other hand, there are plenty of stoners like the ones who boasted to *High Times*, "This bud's so good that I watched the Home Shopping Network for two hours."

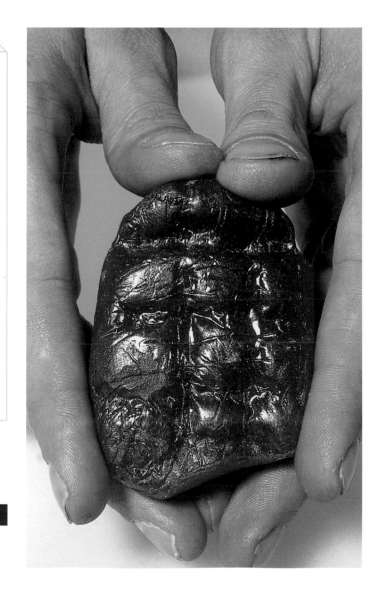

## CULTIVATION NOTES

 **GENETICS**  INDICA

 **GROWN IN**  AFGHANISTAN

# SCREEN HASH

From Trichome Technologies in California, refined by sieving through a very fine screen. Homemade hashish like this is becoming increasingly common.

## Hard Time in the Sooner State

Oklahoma is probably the worst place in the United States to get busted for pot. The state's politics combine the harshest elements of Western vigilantism and Southern Bible Belt puritanism. The prosecutor in the case where grower Will Foster got 93 years was disappointed because he'd asked for 200. In 1992, Jimmy Montgomery, a paraplegic, got 45 years for possession of just under two ounces with intent to sell. And in 2002, an upstate New York man arrested for smoking a joint in his car on Interstate 40 had the $12,000 he was carrying seized as "drug money."

## CULTIVATION NOTES

**GENETICS**   UNKNOWN, PROBABLY INDICA

**GROWN IN**   CALIFORNIA

# CHAMPAGNE

A fluffy-budded hybrid about 70 percent indica, it's well rated in B.C., where several variations have been bred. Grown in California by the Spice Brothers, a low-cost seed company.

## Slap-Shot Smuggling

The boundary between the United States and Canada is often called "the longest undefended border in the world." Though surveillance and harassment at official crossings has increased recently—a pot conviction or even admitting that you ever smoked herb can get you barred from entering the US—the 400-mile line that separates British Columbia from Washington, Idaho, and Montana is policed much less intensely than the heavily militarized US–Mexican border. B.C. buds cross over by air, land, and sea. The lowest-tech tactic is to find a remote, forested area and walk across. A hockey bag can fit 40 pounds, which go for $2,000 or more each.

## CULTIVATION NOTES

**GENETICS**  INDICA/SATIVA

**GROWN IN**  CALIFORNIA

# SHISKABERRY

A cross between the Canadian strain Blueberry and Afghani, almost all indica. From Spice of Life, a seed company using both Dutch and Canadian genetics, which calls it their "most popular seed of all time" and recently reissued it as Shiskaberry #3. Though bred for indoor cultivation, it has been harvested outdoors in Canada.

## Ganja Been Berry, Berry Good to Me

Shiskaberry is part of the "berry" family, a group of fruity-tasting strains that includes Blueberry, developed by Canadian breeder DJ Short; Bubbleberry, a descendant with a sweet, gummy flavor; and variations thereof. Blueberry comes from an Afghani indica crossed with Thai and Mexican sativas.

## CULTIVATION NOTES

**GENETICS** ABOUT 90% INDICA

**GROWN IN** DETROIT

# BIG BUD

A heavy-yielding indica/sativa containing Skunk and Afghani genetics, this is another classic Northwest strain, with buds so big they can break off if the branches aren't supported. This Dutch version comes from the Blue Bird coffeeshop in Amsterdam.

### Stamp Out Ditchweed!

The US government spends over $10 million annually to eradicate marijuana, with the number of plants hacked down, burned, or sprayed with herbicide in recent years ranging from 133 million in 1999 to over 570 million in 2001. Yet more than 98 percent of the plants destroyed are "ditchweed," wild hemp that contains less than 1 percent THC and is thus utterly useless for getting high. These are concentrated in the old hemp-growing areas of West Virginia, Kentucky, Tennessee, Indiana, Missouri, and Oklahoma. Meanwhile, the annual number of plants seized that were actually cultivated has averaged around 3 million outdoors and 225,000 indoors.

## CULTIVATION NOTES

 **GENETICS** INDICA/SATIVA

 **GROWN IN** NETHERLANDS

# WHITE WIDOW

A popular Dutch strain, this is an Indian/Brazilian indica/sativa, about 60% sativa, sticky and pungent, with a fruity, floral taste and buds covered in so many trichomes they look like snow. It can be grown indoors or out. From the Green House coffeeshop in Amsterdam. White Widow won the Cannabis Cup in 1995.

### The Million Marijuana March

Ex-Yippie Dana Beal, the main organizer of New York's annual May pot rally, renamed it the "Million Marijuana March" in 1998. (Black nationalist Louis Farrakhan's Million Man March inspired the name.) The idea spread rapidly, and pot rallies now occur on the first weekend in May in over 200 cities, on every continent except Antarctica.

**CULTIVATION NOTES**

 **GENETICS**  SATIVA/INDICA

**GROWN IN**  NETHERLANDS

# BIO SKUNK

Another Dutch variation on Skunk; "bio" is a European term for grown in soil. Grown for the Blue Bird coffeeshop in Amsterdam.

## Did You Just Run Over a Skunk?

Marijuana smoke has a unique and pungent odor. It's often unnoticeable to the people smoking it, but both those who disapprove and those who'd like a toke detect it easily. For those who don't want to live life with towels stuffed under their door, stoner-folklore remedies include burning incense or spraying air freshener; exhaling the smoke through a cardboard toilet-paper tube stuffed with sheets of fabric softener; and Ozium, a spray used by undertakers to mask the stench of death. The legendary New Orleans pianist Professor Longhair built pushbuttons into his armchair that would squirt insecticide in the corners of his room so his wife wouldn't smell his reefer.

## CULTIVATION NOTES

 **GENETICS**  INDICA/SATIVA
 **GROWN IN**  NETHERLANDS

# FINGER HASH

Hash extracted from Soma Skunk by rubbing the resin off with fingertips. This is the lowest-tech method of making hashish. A more complex technique involves ice water and filters.

## Pipe Cleaning

Several commercial products are available that clean the gunk off pipes, especially glass ones. They have brand names like Formula 420, Orange Chronic, and Grunge Off (which will not erase the music from your old Nirvana, Mudhoney, and Alice in Chains CDs). A mix of alcohol and salt will probably do just as well.

## CULTIVATION NOTES

**GENETICS**  INDICA/SATIVA

**GROWN IN**  NETHERLANDS

# WESTERN WINDS

Described as an "almost pure sativa" similar to Kali Mist, with a Haze taste and high. It flowers in 70–75 days indoors. Grown by Sagarmatha Seeds in Amsterdam, which touts its spiritual, high-energy buzz, "unique Oriental aroma," and popularity among the staff.

## Stoner Darwin Awards 2

In 1994, a Canton, Ohio man passed out drunk in his house, his stereo blasting loud enough for neighbors a block away to complain. Police arrived at 1:30 a.m. and found six empty beers on the floor—and about 150 plants growing in the basement.

## CULTIVATION NOTES

**GENETICS**  PREDOMINANTLY SATIVA
**GROWN IN**  NETHERLANDS

# KUSHMAN'S KUSH

An Afghani-descended strain ("kush" refers to the Hindu Kush mountains), developed by cultivation expert Kyle Kushman. Grown in upstate New York.

### Rooftop Tea Pad

One of the most unorthodox of New York's "tea pads," according to the 1944 LaGuardia Commission report, "was a series of pup tents arranged on a rooftop in Harlem. Those present proceeded to smoke their cigarettes in the tents. When the desired effect of the drug had been obtained, they all merged into the open and engaged in a discussion of their admiration of the stars and the beauties of nature." Later, while studying a group of prisoners for their reactions to reefer, the commission built an ersatz tea pad for them, complete with shaded lights and a radio, in a locked hospital ward.

## CULTIVATION NOTES

 **GENETICS** INDICA

 **GROWN IN** UPSTATE NEW YORK

# JUICY FRUIT

A Thai/Afghani cross that smells and tastes sweet, like Juicy Fruit gum. Developed by the Sensi Seed Bank in Amsterdam, which has reissued it as "Fruity Juice," billing it as a heavy yielder which flowers in 50 to 60 days. Grown by Trichome Technologies in California.

### Legalize Pot in Three E-Z Steps

Like children, inexperienced computer geeks, and the more dogmatic political types among us, pot-smokers are often prone to magical thinking and simplistic solutions. By the ideas some people offer, cannabis would be legalized instantly and effortlessly "if everyone would just plant their seeds," if stoners showed the world that the Bible ordains that we get high, or if people could just be persuaded to call it "cannabis" or "hemp" instead of "marijuana." And if you send $10,000 to this deposed Nigerian general...

## CULTIVATION NOTES

**GENETICS**  INDICA/SATIVA

**GROWN IN**  CALIFORNIA

# COOKING WITH CANNABIS

**Eating cannabis is a venerable way of getting high, and it can render you extremely baked for long periods of time without having to scorch your throat. However, it's not as easy as just sprinkling a few croutons of bud on a salad.**

THC is fat-soluble, so it has to be cooked in butter or oil for some time to become accessible by the body. Raw cannabis contains cannabinoid acids that turn to THC when it is smoked or cooked.

Buds and hash are more potent, but cooking is an excellent way to use leaf. It's cheaper, and the amount of leaf that would leave your lungs a charred ruin if you smoked enough to get high can go very well in food. Shake, the scraps that fall off buds, and trim leaves are also great for cooking.

Dosages are hard to predict, and must be learned by trial and error. Slightly more than the amount each person would smoke in one sitting is a good place to start, but results can vary due to differences in pot potency and how the body absorbs it. In a heavy dish such as lasagna, it's good to use a lot, or else it won't be enough to be useful.

The effects of eating cannabis can take up to two hours to come on. Those who don't eat enough waste pot, but the impatient who eat extra may find themselves extremely wasted. If you err on the side of eating too much, you should have several hours where you don't have to drive, have no pressing obligations, and are around friends who'll entertain you while you're puddlefied. The high from eating cannabis lasts much longer and can be more intense than the high from smoking it.

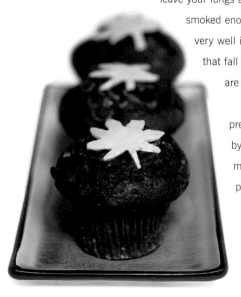

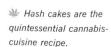 *Hash cakes are the quintessential cannabis-cuisine recipe.*

# Cannabutter

This recipe is the basis for just about everything that follows, as THC is fat-soluble. Butter works best, but olive oil or a saturated-fat oil will also do the job.

## INGREDIENTS

*One formula is 2–7 grams of bud or ¼–1 oz of leaf for a ¼-lb stick of butter, yielding a dose (in inverse proportions) of ½–2 tbsp per person.*

## METHOD 1

❶ The buds or leaf should be crumbled into small flakes or powder.

❷ The herb and butter or oil go in a double boiler, a small pot inside a larger pot filled with water; this prevents the butter-herb mix from burning, as it can if cooked directly on the stove. Cooking on the stove needs the lowest heat possible with a few tablespoons of water added, and frequent stirring. Use organic butter—you don't want pesticides or growth hormones in your food, and margarine, unless organic, is probably made with oil from genetically modified corn or soybeans. It takes around 20–45 minutes to cook and it's important not to let it burn. "Not only do you ruin the high, but the flavor is awful!" warns former *High Times* news editor Peter Gorman, a veteran professional chef.

❸ When done, the leaf residue can be strained out, otherwise everything with it will taste like pot. (The leftover herb can then be chopped up further and added to an "herbed bread" recipe.) Gorman suggests using cannabutter to cook an omelet or for grilled cheese sandwiches, while cannabis oil can be used to sauté a veggie mix, or chilled and used to season a tuna nicoise.

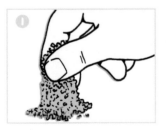

## METHOD 2

🍁 Another method is to put enough water in a soup pot to more than cover the herb, and then add butter and simmer for a couple of hours. Chilling in the refrigerator will separate the butter from the old skanky water. The water can then be drained through a hole poked in the chilled butter. Then the butter is heated enough to press the leaf out and rechilled in a metal bowl. The remaining water is then drained off and what is left is the most gorgeous green lovin' butter! Whatever isn't used can be refrigerated or frozen.

# Ganja Gourmet Brownies

Brownies are perhaps the one dish most associated with cannabis cuisine, ever since the inclusion of "hashisch fudge" in *The Alice B. Toklas Cookbook*, the witty memoir/cookbook published by Gertrude Stein's companion in 1954. This recipe comes from a New York anarchist gourmet.

## INGREDIENTS

*9 oz UNsweetened chocolate (not bittersweet, not semisweet).*
*10 oz "enhanced" butter*
*9 large eggs*
*2 lbs (yes, pounds!) white sugar*
*½ tbsp vanilla extract*
*½ tbsp salt*
*2¼ cups all-purpose flour*
*8 oz walnut halves, chopped*

## METHOD

The chocolate and cannabutter are gently melted together over very low heat or in a double boiler. Chocolate separates if heated too much, so this has to be done carefully. The mixture is blended until thoroughly combined and then cooled to room temperature.

The eggs are beaten in one at a time using an electric mixer on high speed. After all the eggs have been added, the mixture should have a pudding-like consistency.

The sugar is beaten in, ½ cup at a time, until all is mixed in. Vanilla extract and salt are added.

Now the flour has to be "folded" in, ½ cup at a time, using a spatula. Do not overmix. The walnuts are added and mixed until they are evenly dispersed.

Finally, the mixture goes into a greased ½-sheet tray and is spread out evenly.

The brownies are baked in a preheated oven at 300ºF for 25 minutes. The tray is then rotated 180 degrees and then baked for another 25 minutes, making a total of 50 minutes cooking time.

The center can be tested with a toothpick. Some people like it chewier and remove it when a tiny crumb or two is still attached to the toothpick. It's more usual to wait until the toothpick comes out clean, then remove from oven. The brownies should be cooled for 15 minutes before serving.

These brownies can be frozen for months when wrapped in foil. They can sit outside the refrigerator for up to five days if they are properly wrapped, and if it's not too hot. They are best right out of the oven with some ice cream.

# Ganja Oil Bread Dip

Simple, but tasty and effective. From a Long Island suburban misfit.

## INGREDIENTS

*For 1 person:*
*½–1 gram marijuana*
*2–3 tbsp olive oil*
*chopped garlic, to taste*
*oregano, to taste*

## METHOD

The marijuana is sautéed in the olive oil. This is cooked gently on low heat long enough to activate the herb.

Chopped garlic and oregano can be added to taste.

The oil is sopped up with pieces of Italian bread.

# Hashisch Fudge

This is the original *Alice B. Toklas Cookbook* recipe, actually more of a fruit-nut-spice gooball than a brownie. It was supplied by painter Brion Gysin, who noted that, "Euphoria and brilliant storms of laughter; ecstatic reveries and extensions of one's personality on several simultaneous planes are to be complacently expected." Expurgated from the original American edition of the cookbook, this recipe was restored in the current Lyons Books edition.

## INGREDIENTS

*1 tsp black peppercorns*
*1 whole nutmeg*
*4 average sticks of cinnamon*
*1 tsp coriander*
*1 handful stone dates*
*1 handful dried figs*
*1 handful shelled almonds*
*1 handful peanuts*
*A bunch of canibus [sic] sativa*
*1 cup sugar*
*1 pat butter*

## METHOD

The black peppercorns, nutmeg, cinnamon, and coriander are pulverized in a mortar.

The stone dates, dried figs, shelled almonds, and peanuts are chopped and mixed together.

A bunch of cannabis sativa is pulverized in a mortar.

About a cup of sugar dissolved in a big pat of butter.

The spices and cannabis mixture is then dusted over the mixed fruit and nuts, and kneaded together with the butter mixture.

The mixture is rolled into a cake and cut into pieces or made into balls about the size of a walnut.

Hashish fudge should be eaten with care. Two pieces are quite sufficient!

# Dixie Fried Pork Chops

A recipe from North Carolina. "Simple and delicious," says the cook. "Of course, most things you cook with cannabutter are better!"

## INGREDIENTS

*4 pork chops*
*1 tbsp cannabutter*
*salt, to taste*

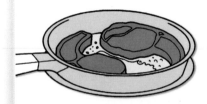

## METHOD

Pork chops should always be rinsed and dried off. Thin ones, thinner than ½ inch, are preferable.

The pan is heated to about medium, then the cannabis-butter is added to gently melt (less is more; about 1 tablespoon for 4 pork chops). If it's melting to a fry, the pan should be lifted off the burner slightly while butter is melting.

The pork chops should be seared in the butter to a slight brown and salted lightly.

The process is repeated on the other side; entire cooking should only take about 10 minutes. The chops should not be left; if overcooked, they will be tough!

# Shortbread Cookies

This tasty cookie recipe comes from a Michigan vegetarian activist. A panelist at the 2001 NORML conference swears that one of these cookies got rid of his migraine, rendering him both exhilarated and coherent enough for public speaking.

## INGREDIENTS

*1 cup cannabutter*
*½ cup sugar (confectioner's or cane sugar both work well)*
*2 cups unbleached white flour*
*1 tsp pure vanilla extract*
*Pinch of salt*
*1 cup shredded coconut (optional)*

## METHOD

☘ The butter and sugar are creamed together very well. The remaining ingredients are added and the mixture worked into dough with the fingers. The dough should not be "overworked" or the cookies will become tough.

☘ The dough goes into a cake pan, about ½-inch thick, and a bunch of holes are punched in the dough with a fork.

☘ This is baked in an oven preheated to 325°F for 50 minutes, until the cookies turn golden.

☘ Best eaten while still warm—yum!

# Growers' Guacamole

The dip that calls for the best, stickiest, most resinous, bud possible. The bud needs to be powdered beforehand (a coffee/herb grinder works great for this).

## INGREDIENTS

*1 ample avocado, smashed*
*1 tomato, chopped*
*1 green onion, chopped*
*1 garlic clove, pressed and chopped*
*cilantro, chopped finely*
*lime juice, fresh is best*
*cumin, to taste*
*cayenne, a pinch*
*salt, a dash*
*1 mango (optional)*

## METHOD

☘ All this is mixed together and to taste, so measurements are pretty useless. The resin binds with the oil in the avocados for a rockin' stoner dip that is best with blue chips (the color combo is lovely when your buzz is coming on).

# Pleasin' Pot Pesto

This goes great with all kinds of pasta, or it can be spread on bread or put on a pizza—a pot-addled imagination can create culinary treasures!

### INGREDIENTS

*Olive oil, a couple of cups, cooked in the soup-pot method for cannabutter with herb*
*Basil, lots*
*Pine nuts (or raw cashews or almonds, depending on taste)*
*Salt, to taste*
*Garlic, lots*
*Parmesan or romano cheese, optional*

### METHOD

🌿 All of the ingredients go into a blender and are whizzed until you have a gooey, garlicky ganja pesto.

# Ganja Tea and "Mother's Milk"

Ganja tea can be made from water, regular milk, or soy or nut milk. Boiling buds in water is not enough, as it won't dissolve the THC. This recipe comes courtesy of the Wo/Men's Alliance for Medical Marijuana, in Santa Cruz.

### INGREDIENTS

*GANJA TEA*
*1 tsp butter*
*1 cup hot water or milk*
*1 bud*

*"MOTHER'S MILK"*
*2 heaped tbsp ground marijuana leaves*
*½ pint whole milk*

### METHOD

*GANJA TEA*
🌿 To make ganja tea from water, one teaspoon of butter is added to a cup of hot water and a bud steeped in it for 15 minutes to 2 hours. The longer it is steeped, the more potent it is. Any oil left floating on top of the tea should also be drunk.

*"MOTHER'S MILK"*
🌿 For "mother's milk," marijuana leaves are ground until they are as powdery as flour. Two heaping tablespoons can be stirred into ½ pint milk—not lowfat milk.

🌿 This is then simmered in a crockpot for at least two hours, ideally all day or overnight.

🌿 It can be seasoned with nutmeg, cinnamon, chocolate, or vanilla.

🌿 A standard dose is ⅛ cup–¼ cup. You can carry it around in a thermos. Additional amounts can be stored as you would milk; for longer-term preservation, it can be frozen.

# Six Pepper Rasta Pasta

"Cooking Louisiana style means forgetting everything Martha Stewart ever taught you," says the originator of this. "Ditch the measuring cups, because our food is like our music; it's full of spicy improvisation, and so long as love is put into it, everybody will enjoy savoring it."

## INGREDIENTS

¼ oz Mexican ganja, cleaned
¼-lb stick of salted butter
Small handful of flour
2–3 cups of cream (half and half will do)
2 tbsp grated Parmesan
2 tbsp grated romano
7 garlic cloves, chopped
1 bunch of green onions (shallots) chopped
Three bell peppers (yellow, red, and green), sliced thin, roasted or grilled
Black, cayenne, and chipotle pepper to taste
1–2 tbsp olive oil
Tri-colored rotini

## METHOD

🍁 The bell peppers are sliced into thin strips and roasted or grilled on medium heat with the olive oil. The pasta is put on to boil.

🍁 The ganja butter is simmered in a medium pan, with garlic and shallots. A tablespoon or two of extra butter can be added if necessary to cook the garlic, but no more.

🍁 A small handful of flour is added slowly, and whisked into the butter until it's a thick, even paste.

🍁 Then the cream is added a little at a time, until the consistency is slightly thinner than alfredo sauce.

It's going to cook down and get thicker, so it needs to be watched carefully, and constantly stirred.

🍁 Grated romano and Parmesan cheeses are added slowly, reducing the heat and adding cream if the consistency gets too thick. Then black, cayenne, and chipotle peppers go in, as well as basil and parsley. This is all cooked over low heat a few minutes more, with cream added if needed.

🍁 The pasta is topped with the peppers, everything covered with the ganja cream sauce and c'est si bon.

# Sautéed Fruit

This is one of former *High Times* news editor Peter Gorman's favorites.

## INGREDIENTS

1 tbsp shake
2–3 tbsp butter
1–2 cups sliced or diced fruit or whole berries (sliced pears or bananas are especially delightful)
1 tbsp white or brown sugar, to taste
1–2 fl oz rum (or other liquor)

## METHOD

🍁 The shake and butter are mixed together. This is then heated to hot but not burned.

🍁 The cups of fruit are added, with sugar, depending on taste, and then sautéed, stirring constantly so as not to permit butter or sugar to burn, until soft and hot.

🍁 The heat is turned up to high, and when very hot, the rum is added carefully. It will catch on fire. After it has burned off, the fruit is left sweet and flavored with cannabis and rum.

🍁 This can be eaten, put in juice, or poured over a dessert (ice cream is great!) or warm breakfast cereal.

# Brownie Mary's Hemp Seed Salad Dressing

Mary Rathbun (1921–1999) earned the nickname "Brownie Mary" in the 1980s by baking pot brownies for "the kids," patients on the AIDS ward at San Francisco General Hospital. This recipe comes from *Brownie Mary's Marijuana Cookbook: Dennis Peron's Recipe for Social Change*, her 1993 collaboration with fellow activist Dennis Peron. (The hemp seeds are nutritious, but not psychoactive.) Her legendary brownie formula remains a secret.

## INGREDIENTS

*1 cup olive oil*
*½ cup sugar*
*½ cup wine vinegar*
*1 tbsp hemp seed, chopped*
*1 tbsp grated onion*
*1 tsp salt*
*1 tsp dry mustard*
*½ cup red wine*
*¼–½ oz ground marijuana leaf or*
*1–3 grams of seedless buds*

## METHOD

🌿 The marijuana is added to the oil on low heat, covered and cooked for 20 minutes with occasional stirring.

🌿 Then it is put in a blender with all other ingredients and blended on medium until thoroughly mixed.

🌿 The mixture is stored in a tightly covered jar in the refrigerator. A little more oil can be added if it is too thick when ready to use.

# Tincture of Cannabis

A 19th-century medicinal staple, tincture of cannabis was prescribed to Queen Victoria to help relieve menstrual cramps. This is the Wo/Men's Alliance version.

## INGREDIENTS

*Vodka (or other high-proof alcohol)*
*Fresh or dried marijuana*

## METHOD

🌿 One part vodka (or pretty much any high-proof alcohol) is mixed to 5 parts fresh marijuana. For dried marijuana, the proportions are 1 part vodka to 10 parts pot. The preparation should be stored in glass or earthenware. The mixture needs to stand for at least two weeks in a warm place to extract all vital elements.

🌿 Tincture can be drunk, used sublingually, or used topically, applied to the affected area.

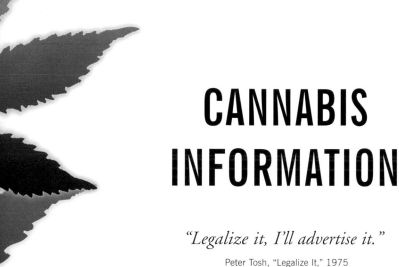

# CANNABIS INFORMATION

*"Legalize it, I'll advertise it."*

Peter Tosh, "Legalize It," 1975

**FEW** subjects are as clouded with misinformation as cannabis, whether it be from prohibitionist propaganda or stoner superstition. It's extremely unlikely that hashish is made from resin rubbed off the bodies of naked Afghani women. "420" is not California police code for "marijuana smoking in progress." Harry Anslinger was not named narcotics commissioner by "President J. Edgar Hoover." And medical marijuana is legal in California under *state* law, but still illegal under *federal* law.

The Web has thousands of cannabis-related sites, pages upon pages of historical archives, cultivation discussions, personal experiences, swirling eye candy, and pot pornography. Some are excellent resources, but many are dubious, cut-and-paste jobs done by ill-informed amateurs or conspiracy-obsessed cranks. Be skeptical! Still, there are treasure lodes of information if you know how to look. The following pages contain our best efforts to summarize the current state of cannabis laws around the world, an extensive glossary of current and historical viper vocabulary, and a list of resources for further knowledge and action.

# CANNABIS AND THE LAW

**Cannabis is illegal everywhere in the world. A 1961 UN treaty (the "Single Convention," since revised) requires signatories to ban the sale and cultivation of it. It leaves room for more lenient treatment of users, but prohibits allowing any legal supply.**

The closest any nation comes to legal cannabis is the Netherlands, where cultivation and sale are outlawed, but the government has officially agreed to tolerate coffeeshops, ignoring the sale of less than five grams at a time and not forcing them to reveal their suppliers. However, in the last few years, the Dutch government has tightened enforcement against growers and made noises about cracking down on coffeeshops, especially in border towns, where most customers are foreigners.

🌿 *While the Dutch government officially tolerates cannabis use, growing it remains illegal, as demonstrated by this 2003 raid.*

Most of Western Europe is moving toward reducing or eliminating penalties for personal use, though. Italy decriminalized cannabis in 1993, and Spain, Belgium, Portugal, and Luxembourg followed in 2001. The Belgian law allows possession and growing of a "reasonable" amount without penalty. In Spain, growing and smoking are widely tolerated.

Germany's courts ruled in 1994 that possession of "small amounts" by adults generally shouldn't be prosecuted, but enforcement varies widely from Berlin to Bavaria. In Britain, Parliament voted in October 2003 to reduce penalties in most cases to a formal warning.

Switzerland was widely believed to be the country closest to legalization, but its parliament blocked a decriminalization bill in 2003. Its laws allow cultivation but not use, leading to a situation where stores sold herbal sachets for "aromatherapy"—technically legal as long as you didn't break them open and smoke the contents.

On the other side, Sweden has the harshest laws in Europe. Simply being high, detected by forced urine tests, can bring six months in prison. France makes it illegal to "present illicit drugs in a favorable light," and French cannabis activists have been prosecuted for selling T-shirts with pro-*herbe* slogans.

In South America, five countries have decriminalized pot. Colombia allows possession of up to 20 grams with no penalty, while Peru and Uruguay permit an unspecified "personal" amount. Pot-smokers in Argentina and Venezuela may wind up in rehab instead of jail, and Brazil may enact a similar law.

Canada's prohibition is eroding. Between 1997 and 2003, several court decisions held the laws against cannabis possession unconstitutional and ordered the government to provide a supply for medical users. The Supreme Court upheld prohibition in December 2003, but both issues remain unresolved while Ottawa ponders legislation to address them. Meanwhile, mild enforcement of laws against cultivation has enabled British Columbia to become one of the world's main growing centers.

Cannabis has also been decriminalized in most of Australia. It remains illegal in South Africa and Malawi, despite widespread use and religious-freedom court challenges by Rastafarians. In Jamaica, a government commission recommended decriminalization in 2001.

The harshest pot laws in the world are in Asia. India has a 10-year minimum for possession. More than 500 grams gets the death penalty in the Philippines and Singapore, while Malaysia mandates hanging for 200 grams. In 2000, an 18-year-old Malaysian got life in prison and a whipping for growing one plant.

The United States' laws are not as draconian as that, but they are vindictively enforced, and Washington's role in world drug policy is that of a self-righteous and belligerent 800-pound gorilla. It has denounced the Dutch policy, and threatened economic sanctions against Canada and Jamaica if they decriminalize cannabis. In 2001, it pressured Costa Rica to enact a tough pot law.

*Lebanon's Bekaa Valley, where this truckload was photographed in 1985, has been a major hash-producing area.*

❋ *Marijuana seedlings in California's Humboldt County. Growing 100 or more cannabis plants brings a mandatory five-year federal-prison sentence.*

Domestically, 12 states have decriminalized pot, but total US marijuana arrests have averaged over 700,000 a year since the late 1990s, with more than five out of six for simple possession. Cultivating more than 100 plants is a federal crime with a five-year mandatory-minimum sentence, more than possession of a pound of powder cocaine gets. At least 10 percent of the 153,000 federal prisoners are convicted pot-growers. Federal law also bans bongs, and pipes can be considered "drug paraphernalia."

The Controlled Substances Act of 1970, the main federal drug law, declares that marijuana "has no valid medical use." That supersedes state laws allowing medical growing and distribution.

## DECRIMINALIZATION AND LEGALIZATION

Decriminalization of marijuana, sometimes called depenalization, means lowering penalties for personal-quantity possession to a civil fine, a formal warning, or nothing, instead of a criminal conviction with jail time. Sale and usually cultivation remain illegal.

Legalization means that sale and cultivation would be allowed. The most likely form it would take would be under regulations similar to alcohol, with restrictions on age, public consumption, and driving. As thousands of people grow it themselves, any viable legalization would probably have to allow home cultivation. Decriminalization actually resembles alcohol Prohibition, which permitted possession of alcohol, home-brewing, and medical use. It's an improvement on the days when potheads would have to serve two years for possession, but it still leaves supply to the illegal market.

## THE DEBATE

Opponents of legalizing marijuana have legitimate concerns about driving while high, use by teenagers, and social decay from excessive bakeage. However, these concerns exist equally—if not more—for alcohol. Does any sane person support spraying vineyards with herbicide and making possession of a case of vodka a felony?

There are three most commonly used arguments for keeping cannabis illegal. One is the "gateway theory," the idea that marijuana leads to heroin or cocaine. (This is a half-truth; while almost all hard-drug addicts tried pot first, most pot-smokers don't go on to harder drugs.) The second, often used by politicians who smoked it in the 1960s and 1970s, is that marijuana now is much more potent. (The supply of potent pot is much more consistent now, but the Thai sticks and Acapulco Gold of yore weren't exactly ditchweed.) The third is that any relaxation of the laws, even letting emaciated AIDS patients puff a little to get an appetite, would "send a message to the children" that it's OK to use drugs.

The underlying motives are cultural warfare and ethnic cleansing. Marijuana prohibition in America began in the 1920s and 1930s as a crusade against blacks,

Mexicans, and jazz musicians, escalated to suppress the 1960s counterculture, and continues against the disobedient and dark-skinned today. The racial paranoia and deep puritanical streak in American society feed the belief that anyone "on drugs" becomes an amoral werewolf, especially when pot is lumped in with methamphetamine and crack. Like the persecution of homosexuality and witches, it's based on an irrational but very powerful fear of the pleasures of unbelievers—a religious war against infidels of consciousness, one that cannot be won unless fear of the master reaches into the most private realms.

However, the *un*consciousness of many marijuana users perpetuates prohibition. Less than 1 percent of US pot-smokers are involved with the legalization movement. If everyone who got high at least once a week would join NORML, the Marijuana Policy Project, or the Drug Policy Alliance, the American pot movement would be as powerful as the National Rifle Association.

*⚜ The National Organization for the Reform of Marijuana Laws, founded in 1970, is the oldest of the main groups working to legalize cannabis in the United States. Others include the Drug Policy Alliance, the Marijuana Policy Project, Americans for Safe Access (for medical use), and Students for a Sensible Drug Policy.*

*⚜ As thousands of people grow their own marijuana, any viable version of legalization would have to allow home gardening.*

# LOADED LEXICON
# A GLOSSARY OF CANNABIS TERMS

There are literally hundreds of slang words for cannabis and the ways of using, growing, and selling it. Some of this comes from using code to evade detection, but much more comes from simple linguistic creativity: The number of English-language slang terms relating to intoxication may exceed the amount devoted to sex, excretion, and vomiting. But while pot-smokers continually coin new synonyms, some expressions have survived for nearly a century.

**AFFY BUD** Afghani-descended marijuana (US, 1980s).

**BAKED** Quite high.

**BAT** One-hit pipe.

**B.C. BUD** Marijuana from British Colombia.

**BEAT (1)** (Adj.) Inferior or bogus marijuana. (v. or n.) A dishonest pot transaction, involving either fake herb or absconding with the money.

**BEAT (2)** (Adj.) Nothing left in the pipe but ashes—"It's beat."

**BHANG** An Indian drink made from cannabis, milk, and spices.

**BIFTA, BIFTAH** Canadian-British word for SPLIFF.

**BLAZE** To smoke marijuana (hip-hop, recent).

**BLOW** (v.) To smoke—"blow a joint" (1920s–1970s). Largely obsolete in US, as noun means cocaine. (n.) British for cannabis.

**BLUNT** A joint rolled in the wrapper leaf from a cigar. Derived from Phillies Blunt brand cigars c. 1983. **BLUNTED** (post-smoking adj.).

**BOGART** Fail to pass the joint or pipe. Popularized by the 1969 movie *Easy Rider*.

**BONE** A joint.

**BONG** Waterpipe composed of a vertical tube with a bowl inserted diagonally near the bottom. Invented in Thailand, originally bamboo but now usually glass or plastic. Delivers a Brobdingnagian TOKE.

**BONG HIT** One TOKE on a bong, often followed by prodigious coughing.

**BONGLOAD** Amount in the bowl of a bong.

**BONGWATER** The water from a bong, foul-smelling defiler of carpets.

**BOWL** The bowl of a pipe; also signifies pipe—"got a bowl?"—or the amount smoked in one.

**BRICKWEED** Pot compressed into a brick for shipping, usually a COMMERCIAL variety from Mexico or (rarely now) Colombia.

**BUBBLE HASH** Potent homemade hashish produced by filtering out TRICHOMES from cannabis in ice water. Bubbles when smoked, and "if it don't bubble, it ain't worth the trouble."

**BUDDAH** Hip-hop term for pot, since mid-1980s.

**BUDS** The flowers of the female cannabis plant; also generic term for marijuana.

**BUILD A SPLIFF** Roll up (British, Jamaican).

**BURN ONE** Smoke a joint.

**BUZZ** A mild to moderate high.

**CANNABIS INDICA** Species of cannabis from Afghanistan and the Himalayas.

**CANNABIS RUDERALIS** Russian species of cannabis, mainly used for HEMP.

**CANNABIS SATIVA** Species of cannabis grown in tropical climates. Grown in the US for HEMP long before Americans discovered its magical properties.

**CANOEING** When the joint burns unevenly, down one side.

**CARBURETOR** Hole in a pipe that lets in air.

**CASHED** Nothing left in the pipe. "This bowl is cashed."

**CBN, CBD** Cannabinol and cannabidiol respectively, chemicals in cannabis whose role is not well understood.

**CHARAS** Indian and Nepalese hashish.

**CHEEBA-CHEEBA** 1970s inner-city slang for pot.

**CHILLUM** Cone-shaped pipe, a.k.a. CHALICE, usually made of clay. Of Indian origin, but used in Rastafarian rituals.

**CHRONIC** California hip-hop term for top-quality pot, popularized by Dr. Dre's 1992 album. "Make my shit the chronic/I want to get fucked up."

**CHOCOLAT** Spanish slang for hash.

**CHUBI** Mexican for joint.

**COB** From Malawi, DAGGA wrapped tightly in a cornhusk.

**COFFEESHOP** Dutch quasi-legal cannabis bar.

**COLA** Bud, especially the long top bud on a plant. From Spanish "tail."

**COLLIE, COLLIE WEED** Jamaican for herb. Sometimes spelled KALI, as in the Hindu demon-goddess.

**COMMERCIAL** Adequate but mediocre mass-market grass.

**CONTACT HIGH** Feeling stoned from secondhand smoke or being around people who are high. Since 1940s.

**COP** (v.) To buy drugs.

**COTTONMOUTH** Dry mouth experienced when high.

**COUCH LOCK** When ganja-induced lassitude glues your gluteus to its resting place.

**COUNT** Quantity for money. "She gives a good count."

**CREEPER** Pot where the high "sneaks up on you."

**DAGGA** Southern African term for cannabis.

**DANK** Sticky, stinky high-quality pot.

**DEALER** Pot-seller.

**DIME BAG** $10 worth of marijuana.

**DIRTWEED** Harsh, mediocre, or impotent pot.

**DITCHWEED** Wild hemp with minimal THC content.

**DOOBIE** 1970s California slang for a joint.

**DOPE** Originally heroin, but adopted for marijuana c. 1970 by hippies as a campy response to hysterical anti-pot propaganda. Widely used in Canada and Australia for pot, but still signifies heroin in New York City.

**DRAW** (n. or v.) Jamaican for TOKE.

**DRO** Short for HYDRO.

**DRY** No pot around. "It was really dry in New York right after 9/11."

**EIGHTH** ⅛ ounce of pot.

**"ERE"** What "here" sounds like when someone tries to pass a joint without exhaling.

**FATTY** A pleasingly plump joint.

**420** Time to get high. Invented by California high-school students in the early 1970s, it spread through the Grateful Dead scene in the late 1980s and then into the general stoner public.

**GAGE** 1930s US term for marijuana.

**GANJA** Indo-Jamaican term for cannabis.

**GOLD** Yellow-colored varieties of pot, including the legendary 1960s Acapulco Gold and the 1970s Colombian Santa Marta Gold. Rare.

**GRASS** 1960s slang for marijuana, now less common.

**GROWROOM** Indoor space used for growing ganja.

**GROW SHOW** Any marijuana garden.

**HALF-AND-HALF** Half-tobacco joint (Canadian).

**HASHISH, HASH** Compressed cannabis resin.

**HASH OIL** Extremely potent oil extracted from hashish.

**HAY** Chicago slang for pot, dates back to the 1920s.

**HEADS** Pot-smokers (US, 1950s–1960s). Buds (British, Canadian, Australian, South African—also HEADDIES).

**HEADSHOP** Store that sells pipes, papers, stashes, and other pot gear.

**HEMP** Non-intoxicating cannabis plants grown for fiber; also, products derived from it, primarily cloth, rope, and paper.

**HERB** Marijuana, originally Rastafarian but now widespread. From Genesis 1:29—"Behold, I have given you every herb bearing seed."

**HIGH** Pleasantly intoxicated.

**HIT** (n. or v.) Puff. "Mind if I hit that?" "Sure, take a hit."

**HOG LEG** Southern term for a fat joint.

**HOMEGROWN** Pot from someone's personal garden.

**HOOKAH** Waterpipe with hoses, so more than one person can smoke it.

**HUMBOLDT COUNTY** Northern California area that was the birthplace of domestic pot-growing.

**HYDRO** Hydroponically grown marijuana.

**J, JAY** Short for joint.

**JOINT** Probably the most common term for a marijuana cigarette.

**KIF, KIEF** Moroccan for cannabis, usually smoked with tobacco.

**KIND BUD, THE KIND** High-quality marijuana. From 1980s Grateful Dead scene. Probably from Hawaiian surfer slang for the best—"da kine"—but resonated with Dead "are you kind" lyric.

**LAMBSBREAD** Legendary 1970s Jamaican strain, now rare.

**LEÑO** Spanish for "log," Mexican-American term for joint.

**LIFTED** High.

**LOOSE JOINTS** Pre-rolled joints sold on the street (New York, 1970s).

**MACONHA** Brazilian for pot.

**MARIJUANA** The smokable flowers and leaves of the cannabis plant. Of Mexican origin, dates back at least to 1894. Possibly from "mariguango," intoxicant, or "Maria y Juana," slang for soldiers and whores.

**MERSH** Commercial weed. (Los Angeles, 1980s)

**MEXI** Mexican pot.

**MEZZ** 1930s slang for good pot, after jazz musician Mezz Mezzrow, composer of "Sendin' the Vipers" and Louis Armstrong's dealer.

**MOTA** Most common Spanish word for pot.

**MUGGLES** Before *Harry Potter*, 1920s–1930s word for reefers.

**MULL** To break up buds prior to smoking (Australian).

**MUNCHIES** Appetite stimulation experienced while high (c. 1970).

**NARC** Drug-law-enforcement agent.

**NCHAIOUI** "An individual, generally having a strongly psychopathic personality, who has become so thoroughly habituated to cannabis that virtually all his waking hours are passed in the preparation and ingestion of it." — Mohammed Mrabet, *M'Hashish* (Moroccan).

**NICKEL BAG** $5 worth, rendered obsolete by inflation.

**NUGS** Chunks of bud.

**ONE-HITTER** One-hit pipe, sometimes disguised to resemble a cigarette.

**ONE-HITTER-QUITTER** Pot so good that one hit is enough.

**PACHECO** Mexican for stoned.

**PACK A BOWL** Fill the pipe.

**PAKALOLO** Hawaiian for pot, literally "crazy tobacco."

**PAPERS** Cigarette-rolling papers.

**PASTY MOUTH** Canadian for COTTONMOUTH.

**PEDAZO** Argentine argot for "piece of pot." "Yo quiero mi pedazo."

**PÉTARD** French for joint.

**PINNER** Very thin joint, a.k.a. "New York pinner."

**POKE** Early-1960s variant of " TOKE."

**POPCORN BUD** Popcorn-shaped buds.

**PORRO** Spanish for a joint (Spain, Argentina).

**POT** One of the oldest and most common terms for marijuana. Possibly from Mexican *potiguaya*.

**POTHEAD** Regular pot-smoker.

**PROPOSITION 215** 1996 California ballot initiative legalizing—under state law, not federal—medical marijuana.

**PUFF** (v.) To smoke marijuana.

**QP** Quarter-pound.

**QUARTER** ¼ ounce.

**RASTA, RASTAFARIAN** Member of a Jamaican-born religious sect that smokes ganja as a sacrament.

**RED** Jamaican for high. "I spent an hour talking to Lee Perry and got secondarily red." —Lloyd Bradley, *This Is Reggae Music*.

**REEFER** 1920s–1930s term for marijuana cigarette, or marijuana. Possibly from Mexican *grifa*; obsolete by 1960s, but resurrected c. 1970.

**RESIN** Sticky, THC-containing substance produced by the cannabis plant, especially on the flowers of the female.

**RIPPED** Extremely high (1970s).

**ROACH (1)** The butt of a marijuana cigarette. In use since at least the 1930s.

**ROACH (2)** A small tube of cardboard, rolled into the spliff as a holder (British).

**ROACHCLIP** Device to hold the roach.

**SACK** Bag of pot, e.g., a $20 sack.

**SCHWAG** Mediocre or inferior pot. Possibly from Yiddish derisive onomatopoeia—"Weed, schmeed, this stuff is schwag."

**SEA OF GREEN** Growing technique involving many small plants, in order to get the most buds from a minuscule GROWROOM.

**SENSI** Rasta patois for SINSEMILLA.

**SHAKE** The powder, flakes, and scraps at the bottom of a bag of buds.

**SHIT** All-purpose noun; European (especially French—"LE SHIT"—and Spanish) term for hashish.

**SHORT-TERM MEMORY LOSS** Inability to remember what you were doing five minutes ago or saying one minute ago.

**SHOTGUN** Putting the burning end of the joint in your mouth and blowing the smoke out into someone else's. Probably from Vietnam War.

**SINSEMILLA** From the Spanish "without seed," seedless—and therefore more potent—marijuana.

**SINSE** Short for sinsemilla.

**SKINS** Rolling papers (mainly British).

**SKIN UP** Roll a SPLIFF (British).

**SKUNK** Seminal strain of Afghani-Californian origins that smells like mild skunk spray. In Britain, generic for top-quality herb.

**SMOKE** Aside from the obvious verb, noun for marijuana.

**SMOKEASY** Clandestine cannabis bar. From Prohibition-era "speakeasy."

**SMOKE [SOMEONE] OUT** Get them high.

**SPARK IT UP** Light that joint!

**SPLIFF** Originally an extra-large, cone-shaped Rastafarian joint, now more generic and used almost everywhere reggae is heard.

**STASH** Container or place to keep pot; also, how much is in it.

**STONED** High.

**STONER** One who is usually high.

**STONER MOMENT** Episode of spaciness or short-term memory loss. From "senior moment."

**STRAIGHT** Sober, not high.

**STRESS WEED** Harsh, inferior pot (Los Angeles hip-hop, early 1990s).

**TEA** 1920s–1950s term for marijuana, obsolete by late 1960s.

**THAI STICKS** Thai buds tied around a thin stick. A connoisseur staple of the 1970s, rare now.

**THC** Delta-9 tetrahydrocannabinol, the main active ingredient in marijuana.

**TOKE** One puff of marijuana.

**TOKE UP** Smoke pot.

**TOKER** Pot-smoker.

**TREES** Hip-hop slang for pot.

**TREY BAG** $3 worth, gone with the $40 ounce and the 50-cent subway fare.

**TRICHOMES** Glands that produce THC-containing resin; extremely potent when smoked.

**VIPER** 1930s term for pot-smoker, from the snakelike hiss made by inhaling. Obsolete.

**WAKE AND BAKE** To get high right after waking up. From Shake and Bake, early-1970s premade meat-breading product.

**WASTED** Extremely high, incapacitated.

**WEED** Pot.

**WELL CHARGED** Good and high (Jamaican).

**YESCA** L.A. Chicano term for pot.

**ZOL** South African for a joint, specifically one rolled in newspaper.

# RESOURCES

## BOOKS

### HISTORY, PHILOSOPHY, CULTURE, SCIENCE, AND POLITICS

**ARTIFICIAL PARADISE** by Charles Baudelaire (Herder & Herder, 1971, out of print). Essays on hashish and intoxication.

**THE BOTANY OF DESIRE** by Michael Pollan (Random House, 2001). Essays on humans' relations with plants—apples, tulips, potatoes, and cannabis.

**CANNABIS AND CANNABINOIDS** edited by Franjo Grotenhermen and Ethan Russo (Haworth, 2002). Scientific articles on cannabinoid neurochemistry and medical-marijuana research.

**DRUG CRAZY** by Mike Gray (Random House, 1998). Lucid, acerbic history of liquor and drug prohibition.

**THE DUTCH EXPERIENCE** by Nol van Schaik (Real Deal, 2002). Personal account of the Dutch coffeeshop scene. European small-press edition, hard to find.

**THE EMPEROR WEARS NO CLOTHES** by Jack Herer (Ah Ha Publishing, 1985/2000). The book that sparked the 1990s hemp movement. Rich in primary sources, but some claims are exaggerated.

**HOW TO LEGALIZE DRUGS** edited by Jefferson Fish (Jason Aronson, 1998). Models and strategies for legalization.

**LICIT AND ILLICIT DRUGS** edited by Edward M. Brecher (Little, Brown, 1972). Objective 1970s analysis.

**MARIHUANA: THE FIRST 12,000 YEARS** by Ernest L. Abel (Plenum, 1980, out of print). Invaluable—still the most thorough history out there. Rare and pricey, but online versions available.

**MARIHUANA: THE FORBIDDEN MEDICINE** by Dr. Lester Grinspoon and James Bakalar (Yale, 1993). The text for the revival of medical marijuana.

**THE MARIHUANA PAPERS** edited by David Solomon (Signet, 1966, out of print). Pioneering and comprehensive anthology.

**MARIJUANA MYTHS, MARIJUANA FACTS** by Lynn Zimmer and Dr. John Morgan (The Lindesmith Center, 1997). Dissection of 20 common prohibitionist claims.

**MARIJUANA RX** by Robert Randall and Alice O'Leary (Thunder's Mouth, 1998). Autobiography of America's first legal medical-pot user.

**MR NICE** by Howard Marks (Minerva, UK, 1996). Legendary British smuggler's autobiography.

**OUTLAWS IN BABYLON** by Steve Chapple (Long Shadow, 1984, out of print). Humboldt County's 1980s growing scene.

**PARADISE BURNING** by Chris Simunek (St. Martin's, 1998). Black-humored visits to biker, neo-hippie, and pot-growing scenes.

**POT PLANET** by Brian Preston (Grove, 2002). Weed around the world.

**POT STORIES FOR THE SOUL** by Paul Krassner (High Times, 1999). Stoners' vignettes.

**REALLY THE BLUES** by Mezz Mezzrow (Citadel Underground, 1946/1990). Autobiography of the musician who was Louis Armstrong's dealer. A classic.

**REEFER MADNESS** by Larry "Ratso" Sloman (St. Martin's Griffin, 1979). Can get personal, but deeply detailed history and full of fascinating interviews.

**SAYING YES** by Jacob Sullum (Tarcher Putnam, 2003). Logical comparison of drugs and alcohol.

**THE SCIENCE OF MARIJUANA** by Leslie Iversen (Oxford, 2000). Probably the best accessible summary of recent science.

**SMOKE AND MIRRORS** by Dan Baum (Little, Brown, 1996). Excellent history of 1967–1994 drug war.

**THIS IS REGGAE MUSIC** by Lloyd Bradley (Grove, 2000). Witty, detailed history of reggae.

**UNDERSTANDING MARIJUANA** by Mitch Earleywine (Oxford, 2002). First-rate summary of history and science.

**WAITING TO INHALE** by Alan Bock (Seven Locks, 2000). History of California's medical-marijuana movement.

**WEED: ADVENTURES OF A DOPE SMUGGLER** by Jerry Kamstra (Harper-Collins, 1974, out of print). Memoir of a Beat writer and 1960s pot smuggler. Worth finding.

## GARDENING

**THE BIG BOOK OF BUDS** by Ed Rosenthal (Quick American, 2001). Just what it sounds like.

**THE CANNABIBLE** by Jason King (Ten Speed, 2001). Beautifully photographed extreme closeups of pot plants, plus lucid and intensely detailed discussion of current cannabis breeding.

**HASHISH!** by Robert Connell Clarke (Red Eye, 1998). Afghani black, Moroccan, Nepalese Temple Balls—it's all in here.

**INDOOR MARIJUANA HORTICULTURE** by Jorge Cervantes (VPP, 2002). "The Indoor Bible."

**MARIJUANA BOTANY** by Robert Connell Clarke (Ronin, 1992). Detailed analysis of the plant.

**MARIJUANA GROWER'S GUIDE** by Mel Frank (Red Eye, 1997). Classic 1970s grow book updated.

## MAGAZINES

**CANNABIS CULTURE**

**HEADS**

**HIGH TIMES**

**GROW AMERICA**

**JOURNAL OF CANNABIS THERAPEUTICS** — defunct, but worth finding

## WEB SITES

**Cannabisnews.com** Current pot-news clippings.

**Druglibrary.org/schaffer** Gigantic library of drug-related documents, including the 1894 report by the British Indian Hemp Drugs Commission, court decisions, DEA and NORML publications, and literally thousands more.

**Mapinc.org** Drug-related news clippings.

**Marijuanagrowing.com** Jorge Cervantes' site.

**Seedbankupdate.com/su.html** Seed companies rated (and slammed) on speed, reliability, and quality.

**Stopthedrugwar.org/chronicle** Superb weekly digest of drug news, put out by the Drug Reform Coordination Network.

## ORGANIZATIONS

**AMERICANS FOR SAFE ACCESS**

(medical marijuana)

1678 Shattuck Ave. #317, Berkeley, CA 94709; phone, (510) 486-8083; e-mail, info@safeaccessnow.org; Web, www.safeaccessnow.org

**DRUG POLICY ALLIANCE**

70 West 36th Street, 16th Floor, New York, NY 10018; phone, (212) 613-8020; Web, www.drugpolicy.org

**MARIJUANA POLICY PROJECT**

PO Box 77492, Capitol Hill, Washington, DC 20013; e-mail, info@mpp.org; Web, www.mpp.org

**NATIONAL ORGANIZATION FOR THE REFORM OF MARIJUANA LAWS**

1600 K Street, NW, Suite 501, Washington, DC 20006-2832; phone, (202) 483-5500; e-mail, norml@norml.org, Web, www.norml.org

**STUDENTS FOR A SENSIBLE DRUG POLICY**

1623 Connecticut Ave., NW, 3rd Floor, Washington, DC, 20009; phone, (202) 293-4414; e-mail, ssdp@ssdp.org; Web, www.ssdp.org

# INDEX

# ACKNOWLEDGMENTS

Thanks to my former colleagues, the editors and reporters of the old *High Times* Highwitness News Team: Peter Gorman, Bill Weinberg, Silja Talvi, Michael Simmons, Ashley Kennedy, and Valerie Vande Panne, who gave both moral support and editorial advice; as well as Chesley Hicks, Preston Peet, Jessica Loos, Trina Robbins, Dean Latimer, Alex Roslin, Dan Forbes, and Mark Miller. I'd also like to thank my former coworkers at HT: Steve Bloom, Chris Simunek, Ann-Marie Dennis, Sarah Ferguson, Gabe Kirchheimer, Brian Jahn, Rick Cusick, and especially Kyle Kushman, who provided valuable botanical advice, and Andre Grossmann, for the photographs. Without the knowledge and experience I gained working with these people, this book wouldn't have happened.

Lee Williams, another ex-HTer, offered business advice and more. Marci Davis reassured me that no matter how skilled your job, you're still working-class and the bosses are out to get you. The activists of the marijuana-legalization movement, including but not limited to Allen St. Pierre, Paul Armentano, and the staff at NORML; Doug McVay at Common Sense for Drug Policy; Tony Newman and Shayna Samuels at the Drug Policy Alliance; Valerie Corral at the Wo/Men's Alliance for Medical Marijuana; Philippe Lucas at the Victoria Island Compassion Society; Michael Krawitz at the Cannabis Museum in Virginia; Sister Somayah Kambui at the Crescent Self-Help Alliance; Paul Krassner, Marcy Duda, Toni Latino (my public defender), Diane Fornbacher, and Trish Taylor of Texans for Medical Marijuana (tea pads and sympathy).

Dr. Ethan Russo at GW Pharmaceuticals and Dr. Dale Deutsch at the State University of New York at Stony Brook were generous with their time, explaining scientific questions. Michael Zweig and Michael Schwartz at Stony Brook, G. William Domhoff at UC Santa Cruz, and Mark Mizruchi at the University of Michigan helped resolve small but important historical points. Kim Sherrill, Arun Gupta, Peter Gorman, Elizabeth Forest, Ashley Kennedy, and WAMM, for their recipes.

I'd also like to thank my too-many-to-fit-on-the-page friends, my fellow writers, musicians, activists, and vipers of the greater Lower East Side diaspora, plus Mikey for the *blunt* instructions and the ABC No Rio Computer Center. Lynn McSweeney's editorial comments are often pointed but never malicious. Caroline Earle, Sophie Collins, and Anna Davies at the Ivy Press.

My family, especially my parents, who raised me in an intellectual, activist atmosphere and put up with me when I was a teenage burnout; Ken, my brother in both biology and writerly commiseration; and my son, Ian, who is now old and educated enough to give me editorial advice worth taking.

## Picture Credits

🍁 The publishers would like to thank the following for the use of pictures. Every effort has been made to trace copyright holders and obtain permissions. The publishers apologize for any omissions and would be pleased to make any necessary changes at subsequent printings.

**Courtesy of State University of New York at Stony Brook Biology Department:** 87B.

**Corbis:** 2, 10B, 11B, 12B, 13B, 14, 15, 16B, 17, 18, 19L&C, 20, 21B, 22T, 23B, 24, 25B, 26–27, 28B, 29B, 30–31, 33B, 36, 37, 44B, 46, 47, 49, 53T, 54, 57, 67, 68, 69, 70T, 71B, 79B, 84, 85B, 86, 88B, 89, 100B, 101B, 102T, 103T, 106–107, 108, 109T, 112, 113, 115T, 146B, 147, 148.

**Andre Grossmann:** 45B, 109B, 110, 111, 115B, 116, 117, 118, 119, 120, 121, 122, 123, 124,125, 126, 127, 128, 129, 130, 131, 132, 133, 134, 135.

**Gabe Kirchheimer:** 55.

**Steven Wishnia:** 35B, 51, 92B, 102B.